21st Century Critical Concepts

Overcoming the Roadblock of Personal, Professional, and Organizational Success

Phillip C. Reinke

Strategic Book Publishing and Rights Co.

Strategic Book Publishing and Rights Co., LLC
USA | Singapore
www.sbpra.net

For information about special discounts for bulk purchases, please contact Strategic Book Publishing and Rights Co. Special Sales, at bookorder@ sbpra.net.

ISBN: 978-1-68235-445-2

Book Design: Suzanne Kelly

DEDICATION

*To those who seek a deeper understanding of the
information they embrace . . .*

* * *

To those who seek to leave every moment better . . .

* * *

To those who make meaningful differences . . .

* * *

TABLE OF CONTENTS

Introduction vii

1. Pre-Define 1
   a. The Power of Agreement 2
   b. Straight Talk 4
   c. Exit Strategy 6
   d. The Five Rights 9
   e. Y=f(x) 12

2. Define 17
   a. The Charter 18
   b. SIPOC 22
   c. Define: CTQs 26
   d. Baseline Measure and Historical Process Performance 28

3. Measure 31
   a. What is Data? 32
   b. Data Collection Plan 36
   c. Process Mapping 38
   d. Standard Operating Procedures 41

4. Analyze 45
   a. The Five Whys 46
   b. Root Cause Validation 50
   c. FMEA, Part 1 52
   d. FMEA, Part 2 58

5. Improve 61

   a. Alternate Solutions 62

   b. Predicted Impact 64

   c. Testing and Piloting 69

6. Control 73

   a. Exit Strategy Review 74

   b. Measurements and Monitoring System 76

   c. BPM Process Control Plans 79

   d. Updated Process Documentation 83

   e. New Process Training 85

   f. Financial Review 88

   g. The Formal Handoff 92

   h. Lessons Learned 95

Post Project Follow Up 96

INTRODUCTION

Becoming a successful process improvement practitioner is more than participating in a conceptual class and passing an examination. It is about a deep understanding of what I have called the "critical concepts" of the discipline. The focus of this book is the concepts of the Six Sigma DMAIC (Define-Measure-Analyze-Improve-Control) improvement methodology, which is based in the scientific method framework of analysis.

Six Sigma has evolved over its existence. Although there have been changes in the discipline because it is based on and adheres to the scientific method, its core remains relatively static. Many of its practitioners have added numerous tools and activities to assist in the identification of "root cause." The business world and the world itself are everchanging, and the methodology has needed to adapt to the needs and challenges. This discipline has been able to maintain its relevance and meet the needs of businesses and organizations, as any supporting discipline must.

Recognizing that every day is a new normal, the strategy of surviving and thriving is to maintain a strict discipline to the basic structure that works and evolve to the changes required. The critical concepts are most, if not all, of the tools and activities of the foundation. When conducted properly, the risk of failure of the project is significantly reduced. Therefore I stress these critical concepts, and I look for each of them during the course of a project or a reasonable explanation as to why one or more was unneeded, because the value of every activity should be questioned.

1—PRE-DEFINE

Six Sigma process improvement has a specific phase-driven methodology called DMAIC. This is a short form of Define-Measure-Analyze-Improve-Control. Each one of those letters or descriptors is called the "project phase" and assumes a specific set of deliverables or activities. Each of these deliverables will be specifically addressed in the project phase in which they most often occur. What practitioners have discovered is that the timing of the activity is not as important as the activity itself. Often, depending on the project coach, the timing of the activity is a matter of technique, or it may be adapting to the need of the situation. In other words when it happens is not as important as "it's happening."

Even before a project is formally initiated, prework is necessary. We call it Pre-Define. There are things to know and things to do that ensure that the project is justified, that everyone is aligned with the effort, and that the risk of not meeting expectations (project failure) is minimized. Let us jump right into the critical concepts and activities related to Pre-Define.

1A—THE POWER OF AGREEMENT

Throughout my career I have seen projects that were complete successes and others that were utter failures. Some of the failed projects were reinitiated because the projects were significant to the companies, sometimes to the point that the company's survival depended upon it. The prevailing thought was, "Some projects succeed, while others fail. Do not sweat it!" I resisted falling into that trap. That drive was fueled by my observation that some projects succeeded the second or third time around, and I dug into why they failed at all.

In the project management world, I was often given projects that had previously failed, and most, if not all of my attempts, met or exceeded the requirements. I wondered why they had failed earlier. Yet projects failed, and I got the proverbial tap on the shoulder. This happened frequently enough that my friends began calling me "the janitor" because I cleaned up messes! Peers would often ask me what I did differently that made my success rate higher than others. I could not tell them. I did not know! So, I started looking at my techniques and methods. I could not see any glaring difference.

During a Closure and Handoff meeting for a twice-failed project, the division senior vice president responsible for the project's delivery said to me, "I really enjoy working with you! What I like most about you is that before you start a project you get agreement on everything that is important, and then at every status meeting you don't leave until everyone agrees on what has been done and the direction of the next step."

That was one of my many aha moments. I began inquiring of other project leaders as to whether they pursued "agreement" in their projects. Their responses to my question ranged from, "That's a waste of time," to "My job is not to get agreement, it is just to do what they ask." I concluded that I was among the minority that believed that agreement mattered and that it was my differentiator. To this day, I operate such that agreement is among the main ingredients that lead to success. Let us go a bit deeper into what agreement truly is.

I would suggest that the short definition for agreement is "a concurrence and/or acceptance in feelings, opinions, or perceptions."

We could spend a wasteful amount of time going into the granularity of specific concepts within, but if we agree that this is the beginning of our journey, we can move forward into more meaningful details.

Agreement is situational. What agreement is in one case is not the same in another. Understanding what agreement is for any given time is important to that moment, and it may be different in the next. Since I started this session with an example of project success, let us apply this thought to a Six Sigma DMAIC project. Six Sigma projects generally follow a specific "project phase" discipline. Define, to Measure, to Analyze, to Improve, ending in Control. Now let us look at what agreement is necessary in each of those specific phases:

Define   Agreement on the problem and the goal of the effort.

Measure   Agreement that the data captured is representative of the real process performance.

Analyze   Agreement that the root cause(s) of the problem has been identified.

Improve   Agreement that solutions have been identified, tested, and prioritized.

Control   Agreement that process changes made will continue.

The act of agreement remains the same across the project, however, what is agreed upon changes as the project matures. Regardless of the activity, agreement at specific points along the way is important. The astute project practitioner knows when there is a change in the need for agreement both prior to the beginning of a set of activities and at the conclusion of that set, ensuring that they agree that the efforts have delivered what was agreed upon initially. When I am discussing the importance of agreement, I normally shift immediately to two Pre-Define phase exercises. One is called Straight Talk, and the other is called Exit Strategy. We will save those for the next chapters or two. Don't you agree?

1B—STRAIGHT TALK

We just finished talking about how important gaining agreement is to the success of a project. At the risk of sounding a bit like a philosopher and a psychologist, agreement as we defined it is important to success in any effort that has interactions. Since we do not live in a vacuum, it is important to have a thorough understanding of the tools and activities that help one obtain agreement from the beginning through the completion of a project or effort.

We will focus on one that I have named Straight Talk. This activity normally begins prior to the formal development and acceptance of a Project Charter. Interestingly, information contained in a completed Straight Talk directly feeds critical sections on the Charter and makes the finalization of that project deliverable significantly easier.

Straight Talk is simply the answers to three questions. They are:

- What am I doing?
- Why am I doing it?
- What impact will it have?

If you and the project stakeholder have cooperatively developed the answers to these questions, agreement is a foregone conclusion. Straight Talk often replaces the Elevator Speech within Change Management. I prefer it over the Elevator Speech because it focuses specifically on the activity, the value, and the impact a project has. When these are aligned, the first step in the agreement journey has been taken.

As I think deeper about my experience with Straight Talk, I have to add that it is not a "one and done" activity. In fact, it should be constantly reviewed and adjusted as discoveries are made or as data changes the previous perceptions or expectations related to the deliverables. Interestingly, Straight Talk not only works well for the project overall, but also for any sub-activity. The important aspect to remember is that the more agreement that one obtains during any activity or project, the higher the chance of support and success.

Let us look at a Straight Talk document. If I can be so bold, I suggest that you operate on the same premise that I do: if it is not on paper (literal or figurative), then it is not real. Straight Talk is an activity that is formalized.

{PM: Insert image Communication Capsule}

This is not a complicated document, and yet it is immensely powerful in terms of its ability to focus efforts of a project or initiative based both on the negative impact that "not doing it," which is found in the "Why are we doing it" section, and the "value" provided in the "What will it do for us" section.

The *what are we doing?* section of this activity in most cases focuses on the goal or objective of the project or initiative, rather than what is specifically being done. The reason for this is that during most projects or initiatives, discoveries and decisions make changes inevitable. Regardless, the goals and objectives remain relatively constant. Project or initiative changes will be handled with a document called Exit Strategy, which we will address later.

There is a fourth section in Straight Talk that is intentionally left blank because the Straight Talk message, unlike an Elevator Speech, is always constantly adjusted to the recipient of the message by including them in the message with "What you need to do." The true power of Straight Talk is in this last section. All projects and initiatives need to recognize and continuously promote engagement. If something is important, every individual that can make a difference, one way or another, should be involved or at minimum recognize the impact that their role plays.

Process Improvement and Project Management are careers. Projects and initiatives are not. They are efforts with specific beginnings and ends. Straight Talk is the first step, before the official leap! Next we will look at the Exit Strategy activity, which establishes agreement on project closure.

1C—EXIT STRATEGY

How do I get out of here?
That is an interesting question!

In some instances, there are laws that require companies and organizations to provide simple and not so simple instructions that guide the person who needs "the out," the literal and proverbial door. An example of a literal one is the emergency exit plan. The little maps that are strategically located throughout a building. These exit strategies are visual, simple to interpret, with little room for misunderstanding. On the other end of the proverbial Exit Strategy spectrum are legal contracts. Many if not all good contracts contain a clause or two that allows at least one of the parties engaged in the relationship a way out. In the most extreme cases, leaving the relationship includes penalties, not unlike the contracts related to marriage.

These examples should indicate the importance of communicating the terms and conditions of exit succinctly, whether it is an evacuation of a building, a breach of contract for nonperformance, or the ending of a personal relationship. For those who know me, I look at documents like these as Exit Strategies. To be truly effective, they need to convey not only how to get out of something, but the expectations related to staying in compliance and the situations related to whatever situation that they were created for when it's time to call it done.

The final activity in the Pre-Define phase of a project or an initiative is the Exit Strategy. Its focus is singular and does not entertain the penalties in the event of a breach of terms and conditions of a project or initiative. If you have not heard this said in the past, I will share one of the major commitments that project professionals make: a project or initiative comes with a guarantee to deliver what was agreed upon. The Cii will remain engaged until it delivers to expectations. That is, if the expectations are clearly defined in measurable terms.

I would bet that by now you are seeing the importance of an Exit Strategy!

I have no intention of committing my life to a single project or initiative. Knowing what defines it as done is important to me and gives

6

me a clear set of deliverables. That is, if it is agreed upon! If what I considered as complete was less than the expectations of my project or initiative sponsors, my performance will be less than satisfactory. Agreement on done is important to meeting needs and prioritizing efforts during the project itself.

Before we jump into this activity, let us consider a fundamental aspect of process-related activities. I consider any project or initiative a "process or change." What is a process? It is a series of tasks or activities that takes inputs and changes the nature or state of them, providing an output.

In our case, a project or initiative takes a current situation and through a structured series of activities provides a change. The change that we provide not only occurs, but it occurs in such a way that it meets the expectations of the project recipient. At that moment, we can call this effort completed and we exit to do another project or initiative.

We need to belabor the process aspect of our efforts for just a bit longer. Considering the output of a process is important because it is what the recipient wants. How do we know what they want? Sometimes they do not know what they want! This is where Exit Strategy helps.

Every process output carries four characteristics. From the project or initiative perspective, they are:

- **Time**—This could be a time deadline related to delivering the project itself or a reduction in one of many customer time-impacting aspects of a product or service.
- **Volume**—This is normally an increase in the number of products or services produced or delivered.
- **Quality**—This is normally a reduction in the number of customer-impacting defects.
- **Cost**—This is normally a reduction in the processing or production cost related to a product or service.

We have now assembled enough perspective to build an exit strategy. Keep in mind that the goal of this activity is to gain agreement. This means that this becomes a negotiation tool. The power of this activity is related to the alignment of everyone related to this project on a set of deliverables without compromise or misinterpretation.

7

Since our objective as project leaders is to gain agreement, the Exit Strategy begins with this sentence.

This project will be considered complete when the following objectives are met:

It is then that we capture and document the details related to completeness. Since we are expected to deliver a change in product, service, or performance, the characteristics of closure are in the four previously mentioned categories:

- **Time**
- **Volume**
- **Quality**
- **Cost**

There may be more than one expectation or change requirement in each general category. An example from the Time characteristic could include:

Time—A reduction in time to deliver (processing time) by 50 percent, within six weeks of official project start.

I see this as change "in" time, "by" a specific time. This creates requirements to be met before the project team can exit and move to the next effort. Let us look at the Exit Strategy document itself.

Like the Straight Talk, this is an amazingly simple document. The power that it holds is not held by the words on the final document but in the activity of creating it and obtaining agreement on its content. Like the Straight Talk, this document feeds the Project Charter and acts as the reference document for many of the commitments held within it.

1D -THE FIVE RIGHTS

It is said that it is not worth doing if it is not done right. But did you know that there is not just one "right." There are "five rights" that must be present and aligned to make whatever you are doing happen!

The Five Rights

I know that you have heard it before. A great cake is a combination of many things happening in the correct quantities at the right time. If a person messes one or more of them up, the cake can quickly become a dessert disaster. Many, what I call "passion peddlers," are out selling "secrets to success." My advice is, "Do not fall for their promises and gimmicks." There are no secrets! Most of their advice is not worth the money they charge!

Success is a perfect storm, a combination of five different conditions happening at the same time. Remove any one of them from the perfect storm and it loses its power and often stops! The Cii team, by their very nature, has been focused on the concept of success since we gathered as a group. Because we are committed to providing what our clients are requesting, we regularly discuss what success is during our efforts, whether we have achieved it, and when it has not, what deterred it. Over time, we refined the concept and accumulated data and observations. From this work, we have been able to categorically refine the recipe for obtaining an objective down to five ingredients. We call them the Five Rights.

The Five Rights are, from a Y=f(x) perspective, with Y being success or the output and the Xs or inputs being the general characteristics of success. Before we jump into the Five Rights, let us ensure that we have operationally defined success and agree upon the output of our process. This, in and of itself, is important to the activity itself. Success is simply "meeting the predefined goals and objectives of the activity." If you recall, we defined a process as a series of tasks or activities that takes an input or inputs and changes the nature of those inputs. We intentionally ignore whether that change meets the intention of the process. These come separately as quality standards or objectives or what we often call CTQs or "Critical To Quality" characteristics. Success is the achievement of those CTQs.

Logic tells me that you agree with that definition, so we can move to the Five Rights. Let's jump right in! They are:

1—The Right People ..... DOING ...
2—The Right Activities ... WITH ...
3—The Right Tools ...... FOR ...
4—The Right Reasons .... AT ...
5—The Right Time ...

When these Five Rights come together the risk of failure is significantly reduced. I can cite numerous examples of fantastic ideas and efforts failing because it was not the right time, or the wrong people worked on it, or the activities were wrong or out of sequence, or the tools that were needed were not available or there was no agreement on why an activity was being done. I bet you can too!

Know this, whether personally or professionally, these Xs must be taken into consideration when working on any activity in which success is important. The astute individual asks:

- Are the right people engaged in this effort?
- Do the people know what is needed to be done, at what level of performance?
- Do they have everything that they need to accomplish their goals?
- Do they understand the importance of what they are doing?
- Is it the right time to do what they are doing?

If these questions cannot be answered in ways that ensure the delivery of the activity, there is a higher risk of failure. The astute leader aligns the Five Rights and only engages in the activity after the answers are all YES. Then the level of risk becomes, "How sure are you of each YES?"

Leaders need to have this higher perspective when it comes to ensuring success. Success should not be left in the hands of those performing the actual activities. My standard for leaders is that they look for ways to remove every excuse for failure (which is not being successful) so the effort has no option but to succeed. Where does a leader look for these excuses? The answer is simple: the Five Rights. We learn this when we gathered data related to project failures and were able to align every excuse with one of the five.

The Five Rights is a powerful piece of knowledge that, when used properly, makes success a foregone conclusion. The Cii recognized this and has integrated it into everything that it does, from the training of individuals to projects and project management, to the development and deployment of process and continuous improvement initiatives. We have also created and conduct training sessions for leaders specifically on this important part of leadership. If you are interested in learning more, check us out at www.thecii.com

1E—Y=F(X)

Introduction

Y=f(x) is not just a theoretical concept used in statistic classes and process improvement sessions to explain the cause-effect relationship in the scientific method. It is also the equation of reality and a representative of the misconceptions that we have. This equation is present in our everyday lives and we use it to survive in this world. Whether we realize it or not, it is used against us also. It is important to seek and obtain a deeper and thorough understanding of it and the consequences of its misuse to reduce the chances of being misled by ourselves and by others.

"X" causes "Y"

The journey to a more complete and working knowledge of reality begins with asking "What does the Y=f(x) equation mean?" Let us begin with translating the symbols and then converting them into words. This provides us with:

Y is a function of X, in its simplest form.

Which leads to:

The output is the function of the input, where the Y represents the output, and the X represents the input.

Which leads to:

The effect (Y) is related to the causes (X) when we convert the word output to effect and input to cause.

Interestingly, I get a better understanding of the equation when I simply remember, *"Garbage in . . . Garbage out!"*

Now let us consider the process that involves going from the acquisition of data to an action. A single data point is not informational. When enough data is acquired and it is consistent, it turns into information. At this point the data is, again, compiled into a single point and it acts as a reference. Repeated references, meaning consistent information points, lead to knowledge. Knowledge is therefore a higher and a processed form of information. Knowledge is the actionable form of information. In most cases, it is the intake of information and the correlation of it to a situation and the response required after the realization of it. More simply said, it is finding the relationship of one or more pieces of information to one or more others, that leads to an action. This is what this equation is saying!

After all this rambling, I must admit that this equation accurately describes the first level in the acquisition of human knowledge, which is simply a description of understanding of relationships. Knowledge is the ability to explain and/or predict the outcome of an event (Y) based upon the (X's) provided. The accuracy of this knowledge (in other words, reality) goes beyond the acceptance of the explanation to the frequency of the prediction occurring when the same condition state is present. The bottom line is that if every time you put garbage in you get garbage out, then this can be accepted as a truth or a fact and ultimately the reality of it.

If this worked only in the accurate acquisition of knowledge, the world would work perfectly and never be wrong. However, for every fact or event, there are at least two equations that individuals accept as truth. The real or correct $Y=f(x)$ equation that describes the relationship accurately, and one or more that incorrectly describe the relationship.

This second equation is one of intentional or unintentional misinformation. It is used in deceptive marketing, such as infomercials. A great example of this is when an advertiser convinces a user (potential buyer) of their product that they will lose weight by taking their pills. They often make causal claims leading the potential buyer to passionately believe that by using the product that they will obtain the desired results. Another great example is experienced when, under the guise of logic, conspiracy theorists use it to tie their observations or assumptions to unrelated conclusions, claiming causal connections. We also do the same thing to ourselves when we make assumptions based on biased observations. Recognizing that there are two simultaneously existing equations is the first step in obtaining a better grip on reality.

13

The Philosophy of Y=f(x) and Reality

Philosophically, the concept of reality has been questioned, discussed, and argued for as long as philosophy has existed, probably even before philosophy was formally recognized. Except for a few fringe philosophers, most conclude that fact or truth is inseparable with reality. Socrates, for example, held that the "Real is the Ideal." He recognized that our understanding of reality and truth was, at best, "tainted." He held that truth and reality existed in conceptual forms which we could only perceive hazily. For example, we can recognize a table every time we see one. However, there are many versions and styles of tables, yet the form or concept of "table-ness" is recognizable in every table. There was arguably no single table that was perfect, some are better than others, hence each table is to some extent or another detached from perfection or truth. There are numerous other discussions and schools of thought. The Socratic/Platonic school is cited to set the stage for defining perfection.

It is important to gain an understanding of perfection to understand that the equation of Y=f(x) can be tainted. The short version is that "perfect" is a 100 percent relationship between an X or Xs and a Y. Perfect knowledge is a 100 percent understanding of that relationship, with 100 percent accuracy. Again, this is just one of many definitions of perfection from a philosophical perspective.

The Psychology of Y=f(x) and Reality

Our entire knowledge base is predicated upon patterns and probability. In the most basic sense, our brain assesses the value of our knowledge on the accuracy of prediction and the risk to our existence. Our ability to recognize combinations of Xs that are risky and avert the consequences Y is the major function of our brain. Secondarily, the ability of the brain to recognize the combinations of Xs that provide pleasure or fulfillment is also important. Knowledge becomes more established when we observe repeated patterns. The more often a pattern repeats itself, the more factual it becomes within our being.

Statistics Replicates Brain Function

Interestingly, statistics follows this same path. Over time, with the influx of data, a statistician predicts the Y based upon correlated X's and with continued analysis and testing. At some point, causation is hypothesized and confirmed. It is then that the pattern is called a fact. This cannot be accomplished in a haphazard manner. Statistics follows a structured and disciplined approach from beginning to end, as does the scientific method, which often uses statistics in support of its fact-finding missions.

The purpose of structure and discipline is to gain common agreement on: "If the information (data) is compiled and analyzed in a specific way and it meets specific criteria, we can call it a fact." All data (information) is not the same and each type requires special handling. Also, the types of conclusions needed require specific analytic methods. If there was not a specific agreed-upon technique for each, individuals would spend most of their time defending their methods rather than celebrating their discoveries! Sorting through those equations is the purpose of a structured discipline. Important to the discipline are the rules that are used to connect the Xs to the Y in the equation. This is a different topic, and we will discuss it later. The criteria for connecting an X to a Y is rather strict and, in most cases, also requires independent confirmation.

Whether we realize it or not, we often look to others for validation of what we see, what we concluded, or what we believe. Our brain requires the same independent confirmation as does the pure scientific method strategy. Nature itself is the developer of the scientific method.

From nature's perspective, reality is an accurate interpretation of incoming data. Interestingly, reality is based on previous experience and knowledge. I was once asked what sanity is, and my answer was, "Sanity is an action in response to a set of conditions that matches a majority of the population and is not self- or other-destructive." This too is another topic that we will delve into later.

2—DEFINE

One does not know how far they must travel if they do not know where they are going and where they are at. This is an Epiphany of the Utterly Obvious. Literal and figurative journeys cannot be assessed without a known starting point and a known ending point. Without them or one or the other, the trip is simply a guess. The Define Phase is a series of activities that:

1. Initially validates the existence of the issue or condition being addressed.
2. Formally establishes goals and objectives for the effort.
3. Formally establishes a team to address the issue.
4. Formally assesses the value of the project.
5. Generates a historical baseline measurement.

The goal of the project is to get agreement on those aspects and prepare all the foundational documents for the formal effort.

2A—THE CHARTER

I once worked with a CEO who said during a budget review meeting, after listening to a lot of conjecture and no supporting data, "If it is not on paper, it is not real." I really like that thought. Philosophically, talk has no substance and is open to interpretation. When it is properly documented, it is much more substantial and less prone to reinterpretation. This is one of the reasons that I believe that the Charter is an important deliverable in the define phase of a DMAIC project. Going a bit deeper, I would suggest that a charter is an important document in any effort of significance.

What is a Charter?

Charters have been around for centuries. They are documents of formal commission of an activity or effort. It is a contract. Early settlers were chartered by a king, the charter indicated a commitment of support from this higher authority. Our charters are no different, except that the support is not a king but a leader within the organization that can fully support the effort. In a more current sense of the term, a charter is a written commitment to deliver and support. A mutual agreement.

Whatever form one uses, a charter presents a lot of information. It is what is needed to ensure a commitment from both sides of the table and the rationale behind the effort. I see it as a document of unwavering focus. When you look at a charter, you understand why I suggest that your first two activities are the Straight Talk and Exit Strategy. When properly completed, they provide most of the needed information to complete this document and more! We will discuss that later.

Let us jump right in and review the components of a standard charter, starting with what a blank form looks like.

TEAM/PROJECT CHARTER

Project Name:	
Date (Last Revision):	
Prepared By:	
Approved By:	

Business Case:	Opportunity Statement (High Level Problem Statement):
	Defect Definition:
Goal Statement:	**Project Scope:**
	Process Start Point:
	Process End Point:
Expected Savings/Benefits:	In Scope:
	Out of Scope:

Project Plan:				Team:		
Task/Phase	Start Date	End Date	Actual End	Name:	Role:	Commitment (%):

Let us quickly run through each element of the charter and the high-level requirements for each.

Project Name—Philosophically and psychologically speaking, when a project is given a name, it receives a substance. My advice related to naming a project is to do so in such a way that it defines what is being done. "Project X" may be appealing, but it then requires additional explanation and definition to be effective, and it is also open to interpretation and misinterpretation. To correctly name a project, it should be a short phrase definition of the activity. A good example would look like, "delivery time reduction," indicating that the project is focused on reducing the delivery time from the order to the customer.

Date (Last Revision)—This indicates that a charter is often not a "one and done" document but a dynamic document that changes with discovery and demand. Every and any change should be documented and communicated with everyone concerned with the project.

Prepared by—This indicates who owns this document and who should be called if there is a question pertaining to the content.

Approved by—This indicates the highest level of authority supporting this project.

I call the top of the charter the introduction. That section introduces the reader to the very basics of the project, and after reading those lines, they can make a relatively informed decision as to their need to continue reading. Next, we move into the real heart of the charter.

Business Case—This is the value statement from the answer to "Why are we doing this?" from Straight Talk. It can be simply cut and pasted into this section. That is, if it is comprehensive enough to justify the project's existence.

Opportunity Statement—I prefer to call this the problem statement. It is the driving reason for this project's existence. It also is derived from the answer to the Straight Talk "Why are we doing this?"

Defect Definition—This section points to what specifically has initiated the call to action. In most cases, it is what is critical to reduce or increase for the project to be successful.

Goal Statement—This section lays out the goal or project objective in measurable terms, such as a 50 percent reduction in the average length of a customer service call or a reduction of rework due to welding errors, from 1,000/day to 50/day.

Expected Savings/Benefits—This simply provides justification for the project or initiative in measurable terms. It answers my question, "Why is it worth doing?" or "What is the benefit for doing this?" It should be the same as the "What will it do for us?" answer found on the Straight Talk document.

The Project Scope is particularly important to maintaining focus. It contains four subsections that limits the project to what is impacted and manageable. They are:

- **Process Start**—This should be the same as the first process step from the SIPOC document.
- **Process End Point**—This should be the same as the Output from the SIPOC document.
- **In Scope**—This can also be called Includes. This section could be anything that may not be specifically within the boundaries of the process itself.
- **Out of Scope**—This is the Excludes section. It often notes areas or process steps where two projects overlap or conflict.

Project Plan—This answers the question, "When is this going to be done?" It is often (or should be) part of the Exit Strategy.

Project Team—This provides information related to who is involved in the project and what is expected of them.

This is a quick review of the charter. A charter cannot be done in a vacuum. I cannot emphasize the importance of gaining total agreement on every section of it. Agreement must be obtained prior to formally initiating the project. The Straight Talk and Exit Strategy helps set the stage for charter agreement. The astute project leader uses these activities to gain support and create a compelling argument for the support and completion of whatever is being done.

Coaching and guidance of these activities are especially important in project or initiative success. I have seldom set out on a project alone. Even after thirty-plus years of doing this, I engage a second set of eyes every step of the way. If you require a project coach, the Cii has them available to help you make success a foregone conclusion in your efforts.

2B—SIPOC

Early in my work as a Master Blackbelt, I noticed that the activity called SIPOC, which stands for Supplier—Input—Process—Output—Customer, was being treated as just another checkmark in the DMAIC process. It was my position that any activity that does not provide value toward addressing the issue and obtaining the project goal was wasted effort and should be eliminated.

Before I eliminated this deliverable, I worked diligently to see if I could link a completed SIPOC to other DMAIC activities, giving it value at least as a contributor to the objective of the discipline. It did not take long for me to see the value of a SIPOC. The value I found was not readily apparent with my historical SIPOCs because they were treated as a nonessential step and not given the attention to detail that they and subsequent activities required. As a result, I became determined to ascertain what level of detail was required to give the SIPOC value.

Because a SIPOC is a verbal and visual high-level process map, my first question was, "How high?" Because of its open structure and framework, it could be created as a general map and provide little or no value. On the opposite end of the spectrum, so much detail could be placed on it that the construction time required on it detracted from the overall value that it could provide. Finding the balance between the two became one of my objectives.

This was a perfect situation for reverse engineering my solution. Like all DMAIC projects, capturing the CTQs early was important. I thought through this using the SIPOC framework itself. I needed to identify who the customers of the SIPOC were and what they required of it. The customers in this case were not human beings but other activities. The list of customers systematically grew as I thought about the information that it potentially held. Some of the obvious ones included:

- Charter
- Ishikawa Diagram
- Cause and Effect Matrix
- Functional Flowchart

- Failure Modes Effects Analysis (FMEA)
- VOC to CTQ to Requirements
- CTQ Tree

I was amazed that this proverbial check-mark activity could play an integral role in project development. These seven customers of the SIPOC contributed to the list of deliverables and the subsequent requirements.

As I reverse engineered the SIPOC standard, I looked at the linkages of information that could be found on the SIPOC and for what was needed by a downstream activity. These are the linkages:

Activity	Info Required	SIPOC Location	Level of Detail
Charter	Process Start and Stop	P - Top Box and Botom	No Change
Ishikawa Diagram	Causes	I - following Ishikawa Categories	More detail needed
C & E Matrix	Causes and Output	I/O - following Ishikawa Categories	More detail needed
Functional Flowchart	Process Steps	P - Each general step	Create Steps at functional hand-off
FMEA	Inputs	I - All inputs S - All Suppliers	Comprehensive
VOC to CTQ to Reqs	Customers (recipents of outputs)	C - At each step	All recipient at each hand-off
CTQ Tree	Customers (recipents of outputs)	C - At each step	All recipient at each hand-off

It was at this point that I realized that every column of the SIPOC linked to another activity of higher value and eliminated the need for redundant work, if the SIPOC was completed correctly. The level of detail, however, was dynamic, meaning that depending on the project, some of the downstream activities required more detail while others required less. I could not establish a single level for SIPOC assessment but now determined the completeness of the SIPOC based upon its ability to link to the other activities completely and without further modification.

Because of this new assessment standard, the SIPOC went from being a "one and done" checkbox activity to a dynamically circular activity based upon discovery. This meant that as discoveries were made, the SIPOC had to be updated.

Although the Green Belts and Black Belts that I coached and mentored were not initially happy with my new standard, they quickly saw the importance of the linkages and the time saved by this single activity being completed correctly. As time advanced, so too did the work that we did with the SIPOC.

- We coded the inputs related to the process step and the input. This enhanced the detail and focus of the FMEA.
- We coded the process steps to ensure better alignment with the functional flow chart.
- We utilized the list of inputs to create a checklist of available input requirement documents.
- We created a list of suppliers and confirmed their knowledge of the requirements of their recipients.
- We aligned internal output measures with each process step to capture processing errors.
- We confirmed all internal CTQs with the customer list.

As a result, the SIPOC went from a nearly valueless activity to one of critical importance and oftentimes the central process improvement activity in DMAIC. Let us look at a SIPOCs and begin to get an understanding of how to complete it.

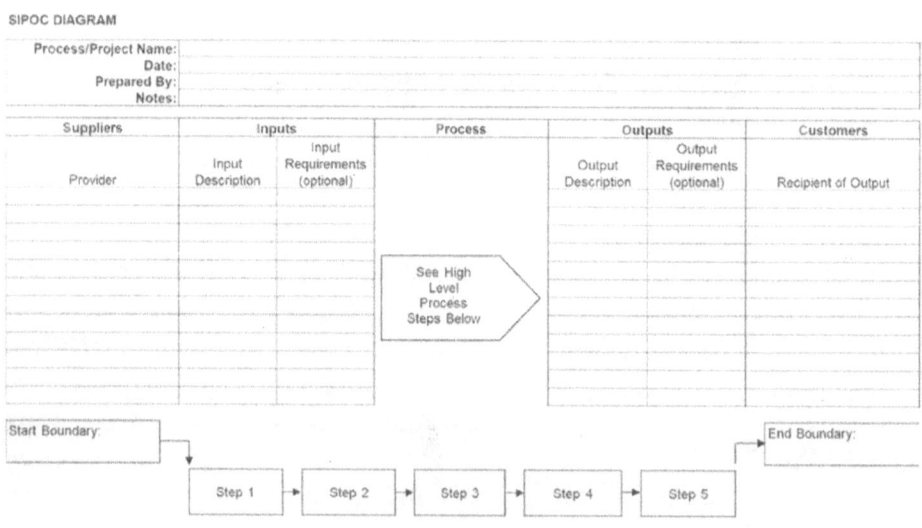

The difference between this SIPOC and the other is simply the location of the Process Step boxes. For those who have worked with SIPOCs before, you may notice two extra columns. The two additional columns are an input requirement column and an output requirement column. They have been added to ensure the activity captures both input and output requirements early in the project and enhance baseline measurement and the development of data collection plans. When this template is completed with the requirements from the requirements grid, the SIPOC becomes the central tool of a project.

We could belabor a step-by-step description of how to complete a SIPOC. My preference is that success begins by taking that first step under the guidance of a coach or mentor and doing your best. Remember that your success and your project's ability to deliver is not on the SIPOC being perfect in the beginning but by it continuously improving during the journey.

All Cii training programs include the opportunity for the participant to engage with a project coach. The Cii coaches are experts who guide and assist from beginning to end. Their objective is to work with the participant, ensuring that they complete a successful project together. This takes me back to my book *My Mentor* and a line from the introduction. It says, ". . . The walk that we are on is a lonely one. The purpose of a mentor is to take the loneliness out of the journey . . ."

Check us out at www.thecii.com

2C—DEFINE: CTQS

This is "Critical to Quality." When that statement is made, I wonder if the speaker truly knows what they are saying. Let us work on a deep understanding of this from a broader perspective. We could play the definition game and combine Webster's explanation for each of those three words and derive something that's somewhat intellectually meaningful. I would rather that we end up with an understanding that is actionable. My perspective is that knowledge only has value when it is put into action that provides a benefit. Memorizing a definition is of little value to the person unless they can use it in such a way that it directs or improves something.

That having been said, it is now time to dive into making CTQs meaningful.

A central equation of Six Sigma is $Y=f(x)$, where Y = Output of a process and X = input or inputs. The equation is verbalized as, "The output of a process is a function of the inputs." From a slightly different perspective, it is a cause-and-effect diagram, where Y is the effect and the X or X's are the causes. The way that I look at this equation is "garbage in, garbage out." Not to belabor the topic, (which I am known to do!), it is impossible to understand the nature of process performance, whether it is good or bad, unless there is some standard. In fact, there are four general categories in which any of the criteria related to an output can be placed. They are:

- Time—When something is expected to be received or how long it takes to receive it.
- Volume—How many are expected to be received.
- Quality—Any characteristic related to the physical properties of the output.
- Cost—The expected cost of the output.

As we consider process performance, these four general categories and the detail within each comprise what we call the Critical to Quality characteristics. They can only be CTQs when they are from the customer's perspective and if they are not met would cause an adverse reaction from the customer, hence the reason for the term critical, and the customer is a true recipient of the process.

CTQs become significant in understanding the true nature of a process that in turn provides a product or service. They become the standard behind the project and the measure related to the success or failure of the process itself.

The Cii team of experts are keenly aware of the importance of CTQs to a project and to their own performance. Their coaching and guidance during projects include ensuring that the true CTQs have been identified and measured. A business or organization cannot survive for very long if they do not fully understand what customers expect from them as a product or service.

2D—BASELINE MEASURE AND HISTORICAL PROCESS PERFORMANCE

Closing the Measure phase of a project with a validated picture of how the process has been performing in relation to the CTQ identified in the Define phase is not only the proverbial icing on the cake, it is critical to the success of the project. Let us look at what a great picture looks like and keep your project on track.

We have previously discussed how important agreement is at the end of every phase of a project. Each phase has a different aspect to agree upon. Since we do not live in a vacuum, it is important to have a thorough understanding of the tools and activities that help one obtain each of these agreements from the beginning through the completion of a project or effort. In this case the tool is a baseline graph. Before we go into the requirements, let us take a brief intellectual detour.

The Great Debate

We will begin by looking at a project from a different perspective. Think of it as a debate. I realize that this is quite a stretch and a different way to look at things, but as we consider this perspective things will become clearer. The "debate" perspective begins with our realizing that a project is an effort of "change" just like a debate. A project is taking a situation from one level to another. Clearly, it is not unlike a formal debate in which an individual takes a certain position, and the opponent takes another. The goal or objective of a debate is for one side to convince the other side that their side is more compelling and accept that the other is flawed.

Now let us move to the project perspective. The purpose of a project is to convince the individuals, especially those I call the resistors, affected by the change that it is important. I call this a "compelling case for change." Interestingly, the goal of this effort is not unlike the opening comments in a debate.

But the similarity to a debate does not stop there! The project itself is a debate. It is a debate with the process itself and with process status quo! This debate opponent is a bit more difficult to win the argument with because its position is engrained. But your goal is the same, that is to get the process to agree and accept the changes and the better stance. Regardless of who the debate is with, it is about obtaining irrefutable information and obtaining agreement that it is reality.

That is enough of the theoretical view of historical data and how it is a debate. Let us look at the rationale behind having historical data and the requirements related to it.

The Goal of Measure

At the beginning of the measure series, we noted that the goal of this phase is to gain agreement that the problem is real, and the data is representative of the process. A picture is worth a thousand words, and in this phase of a project, it is an expected deliverable. Remember that one cannot manage what one cannot measure. The baseline measure is what justifies the existence of the project, and over time it is also the thermometer of success, showing the actual change or improvement. This is the point where the project becomes real. Let us look at what makes a great baseline graph:

- The graph is a simple "Time Series" graph—For a project to be valid, the data must show that the issue or problem being addressed is ongoing and repeated.
- The graph must show at least twelve data points.
- The graph should not contain any other informational data points (beyond the mean). This means no specification limits or control limits.

That is really all you need to know to create the required deliverable. You can see what one looks like on the following page.

A lot of time is wasted creating fancy graphs. These can be developed later when it is important. What matters is the message that the graph conveys is twofold. The first message is that the data show there really is a problem, and the second message is that it has been going on for the time suspected.

With the completion of the time series, base line graph, we will be moving to the Analyze phase concepts.

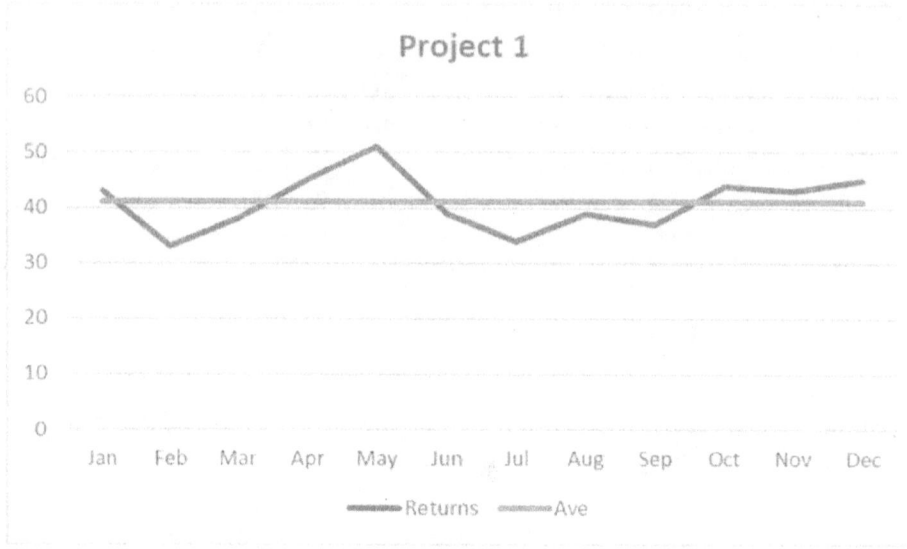

Remember to ask your project champion and all the stakeholders this question before moving forward: Do you agree that the data and information captured in this phase is representative of the process performance?

If they respond with an emphatic "YES!" you are one step closer to a successful project!

3—MEASURE

The objective of the measure phase is to gain agreement that the data captured is reflective of the process performance and that each Y or output datapoint is aligned with the contributing X's or inputs. Most projects focus on obtaining just numeric data and miss the fact that, at best, that is just one third of the data necessary to support that improvement or change effort.

Data exists in three forms, numeric, visual, and verbal. Each will be detailed later. Capturing all three data sources helps reduce the risk of errors and speeds project progress in later stages. This is the time that relentless pursuit and obtainment of data is critical.

Our goal is to show that the problem is real and that we have data that holds the answer to changing it. We are on a journey to find the proverbial needle in a haystack. Six Sigma is fact-based (data) decision making. The more data, the better the decisions. This is when it is amassed and organized.

3A—WHAT IS DATA?

When I ask, "What is data?" the answer that I normally hear is, "It is the numbers related to what you are observing." The fact is that this answer is only one third correct. What is right within that answer is that it is about the event or condition being observed. The beginning of their response related to numbers is only partially correct. Data is a much broader concept, and it is critical to capture all the data sources to effectively understand and address whatever situation is at hand.

Let us start with the correct assumption that data is the information related to a specific event or condition. For our purposes, information of value is that which also contains the reason for a condition of a situation, providing the knowledge to identify it.

During every project coaching session that I am involved in, I ask the project leader, "Have you captured all the data needed to achieve your objective?" They often respond proudly, "Yes!" and show me a spreadsheet. At that point in the session I say, "That is a good start, but you have a long way to go." The response that I get is generally one of confusion. This creates a learning opportunity that I always take advantage of.

Numbers are "Just the Beginning."

Numbers are important to a project and key in analysis, but they are just part of the package. Numbers are descriptive in nature and they may have captured the event in question, but from that point, more and different information is required to laser focus on the root cause. Understanding the complete nature of data becomes even more interesting when one considers the psychology of the project participants and how communication must be considered. Adding to that are the true needs of the project itself. This shows the importance of a complete data collection understanding. Let us jump in!

Although we seldom consciously recognize it, when we communicate, there are three styles or languages spoken. They are not the literal interpretation of languages such as English, German, or French. Communication is the method by which one transmits a message that creates a common understanding of an event or condition. Technically speaking, the act of communication is the transmission of information from sender to receiver that elicits the intended response.

The distribution of the languages across the population is about equal; about a third of each type of style or language is spoken by the group members. To be effective with a group, the communicator must be aware of this challenge and at any given time be prepared to communicate in all three languages. I have belabored the point. Let us look at the three languages or styles. They are:

- **Numeric**—These individuals understand the world in terms of numbers. They live in the world of spreadsheets. They are the numbers people.
- **Verbal**—This group of individuals gains understanding by talking through it. They ask questions and look for answers through verbalization and narratives. These are the talkers.
- **Visual**—This is the "show me the picture" communicator. They live in the world of "back of the envelope" drawings or direct observation of the process. These are the pictures are worth a thousand words people.

One style is no better than another. It is important to recognize the differences to become a fully successful communicator. There is an ocean of research on communication styles and to go much deeper than we have would exhaust many five-minute sessions. Knowing these three styles and the data required to fulfill those needs leads us to a more complete data collection strategy.

Remember that the major purpose of data collection is to fulfill the needs of the analyze phase. Secondarily, a project benefits from its support of change management. Let us get fully back on track and discuss what a complete data collection effort is.

What am I really gathering?

We spent a little time discussing the theoretical nature of data based on the needs of people. Let us not forget that the bottom line is that the data is here for the project's benefit and has one purpose, that is to solve a problem. As an aside, I have often not been able to identify the specific root cause of a problem in the numbers but found it in the visual or verbal perspectives.

What I have found interesting is that the three proverbial languages can act as general categories for the types of data that should be captured to fulfill the data collection needs for a project.

Complicated Spreadsheet

Numeric—This is the easiest to understand. It is important to measure all the Y characteristics related to the failures in the CTQs. This indicates to us whether our output was a success or a failure, meaning that the output either met customer requirements or it did not. Numeric data does not stop with the measurement of the output. In alignment, each measurement has the values related to the Xs that contributed to the specific Y. Alignment is critical. What does this mean? If you recall the equation $Y=f(x)$, the performance of each individual Y is causally related to the Xs that contributed to it. This means that a spreadsheet should have quite a large count of individual numbers on it.

Flowchart—Visual Series

Visual—The are many types of visual representations of a process. There are SIPOCs, task and functional flow charts, spaghetti charts, value stream maps, cause-effect diagrams, fishbone diagrams, and many more. The maps or drawings created as process data should only be driven by the aspects of the process that are failing or potentially failing.

Standard Operating Procedures—Verbal Series

Verbal—We seldom realize that the third type of data exists. It is most often found in the form of Standard Operating Procedures, which are often called SOPs. I have learned an important lesson by asking for a copy of the SOPs related to a process and receiving the answer, "We don't have standard operating procedures." That answer is often the root cause of the reason for variation of the output.

We have now identified what the complete data set is. It is:

- NUMERIC—Generally in the form of a spreadsheet.
- VISUAL—Process maps, pictures, etc.
- VERBAL—Customer feedback, interviews, and SOPs.

As we consider data collection, it is important to know what you need to collect. I hope that his helps. Before that, it important to understand why we are collecting it. I hope our discussion helped with that also. Remember that data exists in various formats. Over time, it will support different needs of the project. Gathering as much as possible and proactively will minimize the redundant work and shorten overall project time.

An interesting aspect of project leadership is that leaders often think that their role is to only control people, but the project leadership role goes far beyond that. Interestingly, projects have personalities and needs, not unlike people. Understanding the needs of both from the data collection perspective will help ensure overall project success. We have covered the most critical aspects of data collection. There is always more that we could talk about, but let me remind you that if you need guidance and assistance, our team of experts can help. You can get more information at www.thecii.com

3B—DATA COLLECTION PLAN

You are looking for the proverbial needle in a haystack, and if it is not in your data set, you will never find it!

Data Collection

The best plans, if not implemented with focus and discipline, are of no value. This is especially true with data collection. Data collection efforts can be frustrating and ultimately misleading if the planning is poor, or the plan is incorrectly implemented. As important as collecting the data is, it is important to know what data is needed and how to collect it without our data collection enemy, bias!

There are many questions that need to be answered during the planning sessions, but of all the questions, the single most important one to be answered is:

"How am I going to capture what is causing the variation in the process and that it is aligned with the output that it affected?"

Let us look at it a different way. A data collection plan is nothing more than the blueprint for a trap that is designed to capture the elusive quarry called root cause. Once the plan is developed, it is time to put it into effect and catch the error or errors that cause the defect.

I know that you remember this critical six sigma concept:

Errors cause defects.
$Y=f(x)$

This concept maintains consistency with our process equation, $Y=f(x)$. A defect is a condition of the process output that does not meet the recipient's requirements. An error occurs within a process. Because a process is a series of task or activities that change the nature of inputs provided, an error could be in the input or inputs and/or with the tasks or activities associated within the process.

During the data collection planning, knowledge of the process is critical to identifying the potential sources of the errors through hypothesis development, which will lead to hypothesis testing in the Analyze phase.

Another way to look at this is that capturing data is like taking a picture of a rare or an elusive endangered species. Often, errors occur infrequently, and it is necessary to be in the right place at the right time. This means an understanding of the process and how it is working is important to getting what is needed to get to the true source of the defects.

Catching the error or errors is just the beginning of data collection. Recording the data is also critical but often overlooked. Data collection is about perfect alignment. Good data recording ensures that the Xs are perfectly aligned to the corresponding Y with such accuracy that you can draw conclusions with certainty! You need to be able to say, "When this X occurs, then this Y occurs, and I am certain of it."

Data collection is about catching when the condition happens, and it is important to catch what you are looking for when it does not. WHY? Because you must be able to show that there is a direct relation between the condition of X and Y, and that it always happens.

This is data collection, short and sweet!

We have covered the most critical aspects of data collection. There is always more that we could talk about but let me remind you that if you need guidance and assistance, our team of experts can help. You can get more information at www.thecii.com

3C—PROCESS MAPPING

Sometimes finding out why something is happening and pulling that hidden needle in a process haystack out of the fray is by looking at "the way we do it" or "the order in which it is done." The only way to find this is with an accurate picture. That is why process mapping is a critical concept. Even more critical than doing it, is doing it right!

Process Mapping

Many projects struggle with identifying the true root cause of a problem because an activity is treated as a check mark rather than given the importance that it deserves. Process mapping is one of those activities that are grudgingly completed rather than recognized for the power it provides. One of the issues related to process mapping is that there are different types of maps. I call them views. The root cause of a problem will often be found in one map but not on the others. Let's discover why comprehensive process mapping is critical to the success of a project.

Sources of variation

Process variation can permeate a process and cause chaos from many sources. The Toyota engineer Ishikawa generalized those sources in his "fishbone" or cause/effect diagram. I consider this a high-level map of the process and often look for this to be a deliverable in the project effort. Those six comprehensive categories are:

- People (including management)
- Process (measurement)
- Methods
- Machinery (technology)
- Materials
- Mother Nature

He created this simple diagram to represent the relation of cause to effect and the contribution to the output. It looks like this:

Below-average team performance

The information can be used to consolidate information from the SIPOC. I also suggest that this activity is populated using information provided by the Fail-Mode-Effects-Analysis (FMEA) and reviewed by a group of Subject Matter Experts (SMEs) who have direct experience with the process. The most frequent failure in this mapping activity is that success is claimed too soon! In the diagram, you can see subcategories. These are more specific than just blaming the errors on people. I call this level of detail a level three (L-3) drill down. In most cases, one or two more levels of detail are required to get to the true root variation. This parallels the strategy afforded by the Five-Whys technique. We will discuss this technique later.

Traditional Mapping

If you recall that a process is ". . . series of tasks and activities that receive inputs and change the nature or state of them, providing an output to a recipient . . ." The Ishikawa diagram is a nontraditional way of mapping the flow of contribution of potential variation that may or may not affect the output. Its power should never be underestimated.

Other mapping methods document the tasks themselves or the decisions, to name a few. Let us look at them:

Task Level Map

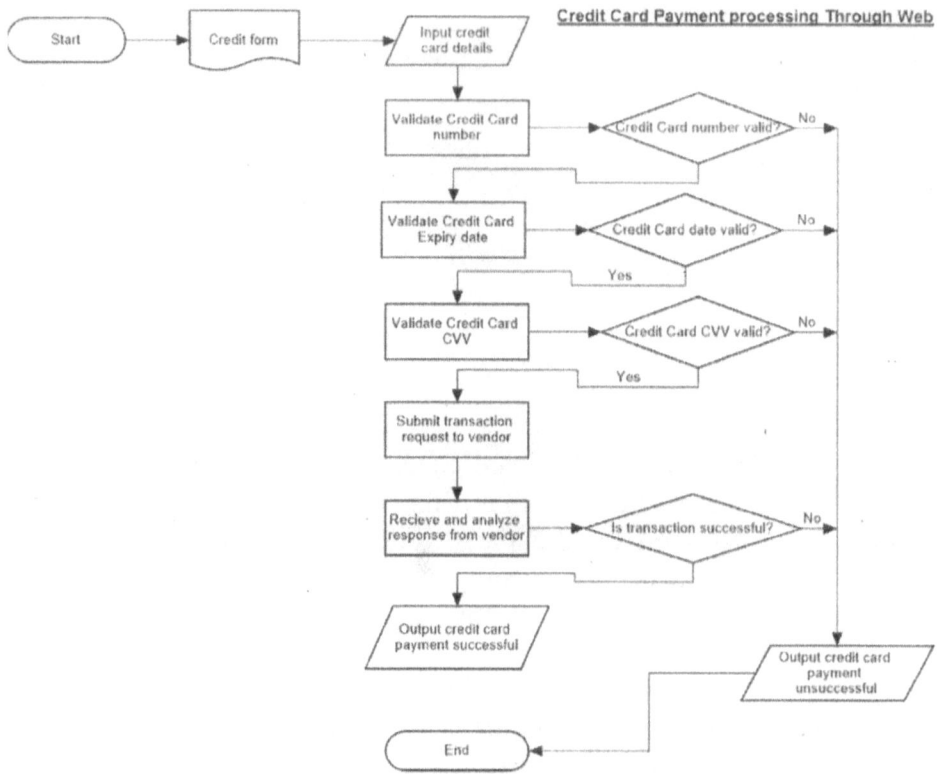

The task level flow diagram conveys five important aspects of a process and the contribution of variation to the output. They are:

- Process start
- Tasks or activities
- Decisions
- Transfers
- Process end

There are multiple levels of this process diagram. This diagram is a high-level map. This means that details are often consolidated in the boxes and specific decisioning details are contained in the diamonds. More detail may be needed with these maps. I often guide diagram efforts to create details for each block with separate maps or standard operating procedures. The sources of failures and variation are found deeper in the details on these maps. To make them powerful, drill down guided by data is important.

Functional Flow Map

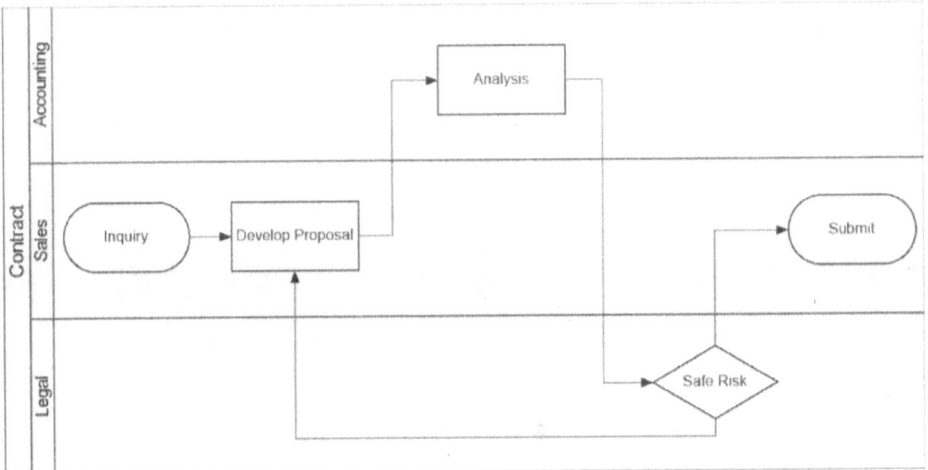

The third process diagram or map that we will review is called a functional flow map. It is often called a "swim lane map" because it has specific lanes like an Olympic racing pool. This diagram assists in the identification of errors or variation due to transfers or handoffs from one department or function to another. The specific symbols are often task level flow maps. Important is the review of the arrows or transfers. These transfers or handoffs are often the source of the error. I pay the closest attention whenever an arrow or transfer crosses a line from one department or function to another.

This is a quick review of process documentation in the form of diagramming or mapping. I cannot overemphasize the importance of this data source in the identification of the root cause of the issue being addressed. It also assists on gaining agreement that the data is representative of the process, the goal, and objective of the measure phase. Remember that agreement must be obtained prior to formally moving to the next phase of the project.

Coaching and guidance of this activity are especially important to project success. I have seldom set out on a project alone. Even after thirty-plus years of doing this, I engage a second set of eyes every step of the way. If you require a project coach, the Cii has them available to help you make success a foregone conclusion in your efforts.

3D—STANDARD OPERATING PROCEDURES

Often, I found the root cause of an issue or the source of variation when I did not find these:

Standard Operating Procedures

Whether it is a production or a service environment, Standard Operating Procedures (SOPs) are critical to ensuring that sources of variation are controlled or eliminated. When I am gathering data, I ask two simple questions:

1. "How do you do that?"
2. "Does everyone do it that way?"

I have received answers across the spectrum. They include:

- What is an SOP?
- No, we do not believe in SOPs.
- I think that we have them, but I have never been told to use them.
- We have them, but I have no idea where they are.
- Yes, we have them, but I have not looked at them in years.
- Yes, we have them, but things have changed so much since they were written.
- Yes, we have them, and if we did not follow them, we would be in big trouble.

Those answers will point to whether the problems lie within specific tasks or activities of people. Remember that the scientific method is about removing everything that is not what you are looking for, like taking away all of the hay from the haystack, leaving only the needle. Asking these questions during the data collection phase of the project is important to reducing the list to the things that matter.

43

A Different Form of Data

Let us go a bit deeper into how the answers to those questions guide data collection. Although the answers vary considerably, the value is binary. If you recall from the discussion about the different kinds of data, SOPs are the primary source of verbal data. They are the written rules of engagement that everyone in the process must follow according to their role.

- If a SOP exists but is not followed, variation often occurs with whatever task or activity is being conducted.
- If a SOP does not exist, variation is a given.
- If a SOP exists and is followed, then the best attempt at controlling variation is minimized.

Whatever the case, whether a SOP exists or does not, the task or activity may be the source of variation. The use or misuse of the SOP is written documentation related to what happens or is expected to happen.

There is no Standard for Standard Operating Procedures

I have come across and seen SOPs in as many different formats as the number of companies that I have worked within. Form and format do not matter. Some are digital, allowing for quick access from a workstation. Others are printed and bound into reference books. Still others are check sheets. Whatever the format may be, the use of them as a control is an important step.

Capturing or not capturing the verbal data related to the process being worked on is nearly as important as the other forms of data. Often it is very directive in identifying the source or sources of variation or failure. SOPs will again rise in importance in the Control phase of the project when the existing ones will be modified and communicated to the appropriate individuals, and measures of compliance will be developed and maintained to ensure they are being followed or new ones developed.

We have covered the most critical aspects of data collection. There is always more that we could talk about but let me remind you that if you need guidance and assistance, our team of experts can help. You can get more information at www.thecii.com

4—ANALYZE

This is the phase where the rubber meets the road! The data obtained in the prior phase combined with the information from the define phase allows for the generation of hypotheses that are subsequently tested using various analytic methods as determined by the data and the actual objective of the analysis.

The objective of this phase is to gain agreement that the source or sources of the variation has been identified. Most projects stall in this phase. These stalls have been called analysis paralysis, and that term is fitting. Remember that we are using the scientific method. Until a theory is independently confirmed it remains a theory. When an independent source identifies and confirms the same hypothesis, it moves toward fact.

The Analyze phase is about converting data into fact. This is the shortest path to agreement. It is easy to gain agreement if you can show that you have identified it and two or three others confirmed it independently.

4A—THE FIVE WHYS

Mother Nature has a way of finding the most efficient and effective way of achieving its objectives. We can take a lesson from it in Continuous Improvement by relentlessly asking "Why?"

The Five Whys

Although not intentional, the scientific method is based on a behavior common to three- to five-year-old children! Let us see what that behavior is. At around three years of age, an internal switch turns on and a child becomes a learning machine. It is said that a child learns much of what is required to take them to adulthood in a period of about two years! If that is truly the case, they have a lot to learn in a short period of time. Nature has provided us with a gift that helps us achieve that knowledge acquisition challenge with amazingly consistent performance. It has been called the Five Whys. If you do not already know why it is called that, I will explain:

Around the age of three, a child enters, what has been called the age of accelerated knowledge acquisition. It is when the individual creates an understanding causal connection or an understanding behind the existence of things and events. It is at this age that learning reigns supreme. To that end, they need to understand why things happen. For those who have or have had children, they will remember them asking why, not once, but numerous times on the same subject. What I found consistent across my children and those of all my friends and acquaintances was that they asked why four or five times and then stopped! Not once did they continue to ask that question beyond five! I asked why.

Interestingly, Mother Nature was unavailable for comment, so I had to find other ways to ascertain the rationale behind asking why more than once. Here is what I found:

- The first time the question why is asked, the answer may be related to the situation in question. It does not fully lead to the foundational reason behind the occurrence.

- The second time the question is asked concerns general process, but still not the true reason.
- Questions three, four, and five drive to the specific reason of what is being questioned.

Interestingly, after the fourth or fifth why, the answer becomes circular or can go no further. Nature, in its striving for efficiency, has found that questioning beyond five has little or no value. It has programmed us to stop there and move on to learning another thing.

The end of my questioning found that it takes four or five whys to get to the root cause or true explanation of the reason for questioning. Why Five" was answered by learning that after that number there is little, or no value added to the effort. Five Whys is simultaneously effective and efficient.

Scientific Method

I had made the claim that the scientific method parallels the Five Whys, and that is partially true. One method of getting to the answer to a hypothesis is through an analytic strategy called segmentation and stratification. This methodology takes a large data set of Y occurrences aligned with the corresponding X's. The data is segmented between the Y data that exhibits the characteristic and the Y data that does not. The only conclusion that can be drawn from this level of questioning is that sometimes it happens and other times it does not. Stratifying the data further by grouping the X's by a condition or to obtain the value or value range allows further drill down until a specific relationship is identified. Oftentimes this takes analysis that drills four more levels of data deep to obtain the answer sought.

It is strange how this parallels the Five Whys technique. The only explanation that I have for this is that there are certain universal truths that apply across the spectrum of information, not unlike that truth that a piece of paper cannot be folded more than seven times and the fact that some schools of physics use this concept to describe the nature of the universe itself.

Knowing that the Five Whys is an effective and efficient technique that is inherent in human learning, and combining that with data set, we can confidently move into the Analyze phase of the project. This is a general strategy and not applicable across the board. Other analytical techniques may be required, but we are looking at this because I have found it highly effective in most root cause efforts.

Five Whys and Business Process

In my work developing Business Process Management or BPM, an area that is worth noting is that most organizations and processes are four to five levels deep from the output level to the individual activity level. This aligns perfectly with asking why five times. An example of this question that can be aligned with data follows:

Customer Complaints

1. **Why are customers complaining?**
   The most frequent complaint is that they are not happy with the delivery time of our service.

2. **Why are they not happy with the delivery time?**
   It is always late compared with their expectations.

3. **Why do they have a delivery expectation?**
   We tell them when they should expect it.

4. **Why do we tell them a delivery time that we know we cannot achieve?**
   Because this is what we are scripted to provide.

5. **Why is this scripted?**
   This is important to maintain consistency. Our processes have changed, but the script has not been updated.

In this scenario, the root cause of customer complaints became apparent only after drilling down five layers into the problem. In most cases, data can be obtained to support the analysis. Simply asking why five times has been directionally advantageous in the analysis of the issue and will often lead to a solution.

Five Whys is a powerful strategy in root cause analysis and should not be underestimated. As you develop your data collection plan, this should be considered. Many projects are forced to return to the measure phase because they compiled an inadequate amount of data to lead to the root cause. As I have previously noted, we are looking for the proverbial needle in a haystack, and it is often found using Five Whys.

4B—ROOT CAUSE VALIDATION

Nothing matters if you cannot prove that you found the needle in a haystack. Focusing on validating the root cause is critical to a successful project. Everything else is just a stab in the dark!

The foundation of and the discipline found within the methodology of Six Sigma is the scientific method. It begins with the accumulation of data, moves to the formation of hypotheses based on the data, and then, using the data, tests and isolates the data to point to the potential root cause. Many mistakenly claim victory at this point in the project. However, the scientific method would say to these individuals that they only have a credible theory until it is independently replicated and validated. Fact does not arise in the scientific method until two or more separate entities see the same thing!

One of the tenets of statistics is, "correlation does not prove causation." This means that just because the data shows that a change in the X has either a direct or inverse relationship to Y, the only thing that can be claimed is that the state of X is a predictor of the Y. That is until the relationship is tested and confirmed. This is the reason that true Six Sigma practitioners are relentless in being fact-based.

First Root Cause, Then Validation

The question asked at this point is: "How does someone validate the root cause beyond a shadow of a doubt?" The statistical answer is simple, but it begins with agreement on what a shadow of doubt means.

- From a statistical viewpoint, it means that it has a relationship probability equal to or more than a predetermined value. The generally accepted standard is the frequency of occurrence is more than 95 percent. This means that the relationship occurs more than 95 percent of the time. Statisticians have a value that they use called the p-value. It is represented by indicating one minus the amount of correlation. This looks like $p <= 0.05$. Which means that the data change is 95 percent or more related.

- From a practical viewpoint it means that you have evidence, such as a trial that there is a causal relationship between the X or Xs and the Y. This will later be confirmed in an actual pilot during the Improve phase of a project. Proactive consideration pertaining from the potential challenge to the causality of the relationship will go a long way to achieving agreement, not only in this phase, but also in the next phase.

The important thing to remember is that effective process improvement projects go beyond the numbers, which are used to communicate with the numeric communicators. Root cause should be validated in ways that the verbal and visual communicators hear. I will leave it up to you to find ways to do that. I would suggest that whatever strategies are used it starts with asking the stakeholders this question:

"What would convince you that there is a causal link between X and Y?"

The answer to this question will help guide you to how you will show that changing what you have found can make a difference. Exiting this phase of the project becomes easier when those who need to agree are behind the data, the analysis, and the conclusions.

4C—FMEA, PART 1

What could possibly go wrong? Often the last words said before a major failure!

When it comes to predicting all the possibilities, "Have you thought of everything?" is a scary question to answer unless you have used the Swiss Army knife of Six Sigma. It is officially known as the Failure Modes Effect Analysis, shortened to FMEA. Like any tool, ensuring that it is used correctly adds to the success equation of a project and the confidence to answer that question, "YES!"

FMEA

The FMEA is not a new tool. It was developed by the US Army to analyze and prioritize the risks related to warfare as far back as World War 2 and it was central to the D-Day Invasion. It went on to be used to this day, changing little from its original form.

The FMEA grasped the true nature of $Y=f(x)$ in that it aligns a failure or defect in the output to an error in an input. The important characteristic is that it assigns a risk/probability value to every input failure. This allows potential issues to be addressed from highest to lowest risk. The beauty of the FMEA is that it succinctly defines risk in terms of the Frequency of it occurring multiplied by the Severity of each occurrence multiplied by the ability to Detect it prior to its impact on the output. They call this value the Risk Priority Number or RPN. The equation looks like this:

RPN = Frequency X Severity X Detectability

Developing the risk for any given input failure is the easy part! The second easiest effort is creating a list of all the inputs. The most difficult effort is identifying all the possible ways that an input can fail.

I have a time-tested FMEA success formula that I will share with you. The interesting thing is that success in developing a FMEA that answers the question "Did you think of everything" does not start with the FMEA. It starts with the SIPOC! I warned you in an earlier discussion that the SIPOC was important and here is another instance in which it contributes just what is needed to make the FMEA successful.

I know that you remember that SIPOC represents five lists.

Supplier—Input—Process—Output—Customer

If the SIPOC has captured all the relevant information, it will simply be a matter of transferring the data from that activity to the FMEA. The specific data, if you have not already guessed it, is the Inputs as they are aligned with each process step.

Let us divert, somewhat, from the SIPOC discussion and identify what could go wrong with an input. If it is not what was needed, it is a defect, in terms of it being an output from a supplier. If you recall, there are only four general CTQ categories. They are:

- Time
- Volume
- Quality
- Cost

I intentionally did not define each of those categories because the specific definition will vary with the item input. Next, since we are in a generalizing frame of mind, let us now look at what characteristic each of the quality categories can possess that may lead to a failure in the output. Throughout my career I could only find three! They are:

- **Too much**
- **Too little**
- **Not at all**

These are, again, general descriptions that can be adapted specifically to the input. At this point you may ask, "Why are we chasing down this path?" The reason is that to answer the question "Have you thought of everything?" you must have entertained every logical and illogical possibility. This takes us to something that I learned in a philosophy of logic class: a logical possibility chart. Let us start with calculating the number of logical possibilities there are for a single input. For every input it can fail three ways related to time and three ways related to volume, and three ways for the other two. We can add them up or multiply, it is your choice. Whatever you choose, it will come out to twelve possible failure modes for each input. The message here is that for each input, if there are twelve failure states generated for each input, you can be confident that you have thought of everything logical and illogical.

Next, we must challenge the comprehensive nature of our SIPOC by asking the question, "Does it capture all of the inputs?" The tool that I utilize in this assessment is the Ishikawa or fishbone diagram. Ishikawa was the engineer who developed this way of decomposing the causes related to six general categories into which every input can be categorized. They are:

- **People**
- **Materials**
- **Machinery**
- **Management**
- **Methods**
- **(Mother Nature) Environmental**

Let us use the Ishikawa concept to assess the SIPOC, which in turn feeds the FMEA. The fishbone is primarily used to assess cause/effect related to an unwanted defect caused by a specific failure with an input. We can also use it to assess the input dependencies of an intended outcome, ignoring, at this point, whether or not the outcome met CTQs. To do so, each specific process step box, under the P in the SIPOC analysis, becomes a head of the fish. If the SIPOC has five generalized process steps, there will be five fishbone diagrams.

The brilliance of the fishbone shines at this point! Ishikawa defined six categories that are basically all-inclusive. Using the categorical groupings, we then assess the "I" column of the SIPOC to ascertain if every relevant input was included. Most often, I find that People and Management have been excluded from the SIPOC, yet human error and management misdirection are the most frequent source of errors. Once the SIPOC's input column has been confirmed as comprehensive, this will be used to populate the FMEA. I am still awed by this exercise! The fishbone diagram looks something like this:

Fishbone or Ishikawa Diagram

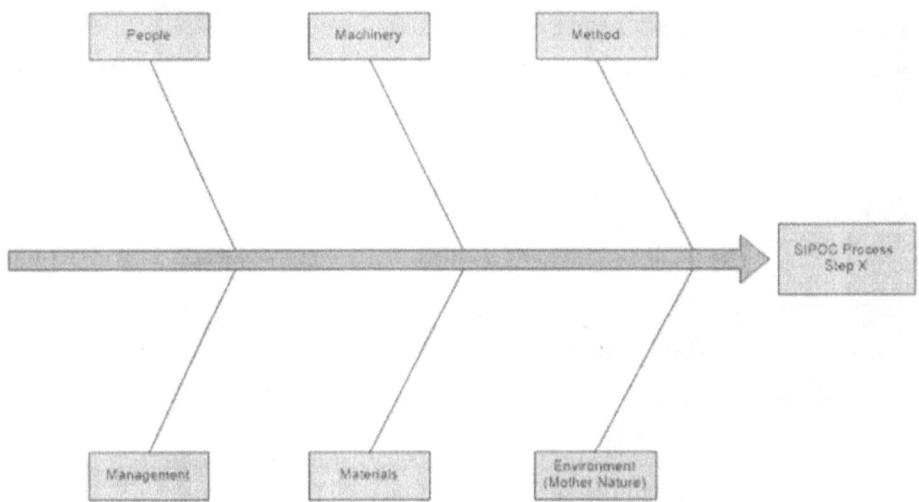

To ensure no misunderstandings, the fishbone analysis is repeated for each process step in the SIPOC.

Now it is time to begin filling in the FMEA. We will start with the first four columns, because the success of a FMEA depends on these being properly completed. *(See next page.)*

This is just the possible failures of the first input in the first step of the process. If you counted them, you got twelve. Some of the failures may not be possible. They will remain on the FMEA, and I will show you what to do with them later. Remember that the Potential Failure Effects is the starting point from which more relevant detail is created. Examples may include:

- **LINE ONE: "Payment Received—Volume—Too Little," which is edited to read, "Payment Received—Volume— Payment Coupon Missing."**

Process Step	Key Process Input	Potential Failure Mode	Potential Failure Effects
ID the process steps	ID the Key Process Inputs?	ID the ways the Key Inputs can go wrong?	What is the impact on the Key Output Variables (Customer Requirements) or internal requirements?
Process Step 1	Payment Received	Volume	Too little
Process Step 1	Payment Received	Volume	Too much
Process Step 1	Payment Received	Volume	Not at all
Process Step 1	Payment Received	Quality	Too little
Process Step 1	Payment Received	Quality	Too much
Process Step 1	Payment Received	Quality	Not at all
Process Step 1	Payment Received	Time	Too little
Process Step 1	Payment Received	Time	Too much
Process Step 1	Payment Received	Time	Not at all
Process Step 1	Payment Received	Cost	Too little
Process Step 1	Payment Received	Cost	Too much
Process Step 1	Payment Received	Cost	Not at all

- **LINE FOUR: "Payment Received—Quality—Too Little, which is edited to read, "Payment Received—Volume—Missing Account Number (or information)."**

I know that you see how each failure (error) can be customized to the common ones that occur in the process. Just to reiterate, many times the logical possibilities cannot occur. It is important to develop each of these combinations. I have often experienced the root cause of an issue being found in a combination that the process owners did not believe could happen.

I bet you just realized that if you have a good SIPOC, you do not require a meeting to create a FMEA, and you are totally correct. The first four columns of a comprehensive FMEA can be created using the input column of a SIPOC. You probably realized that given the number of inputs that are on a comprehensive SIPOC, the number of lines on the FMEA is huge! Again, I have to say that you are, again, absolutely correct. Finally, you probably thought that there a lot of other columns that need to be completed before a practitioner can call it complete, and I again applaud you for your intuitiveness. Sadly, I have used up the allotted time, but we will address the rest of the FMEA in the next session.

4D—FMEA PART 2

Building an effective FMEA is not an easy task. Harder even than constructing it is gaining agreement on its accuracy and representation of the process risks. A FMEA is worthless unless everyone agrees with its results and prioritizations. After attaining that, the stage is set for great and wonderful things!

If you remember from part one, the FMEA is not a new tool. It was developed by the US Army to analyze and prioritize risk way back in World War 2 and the D-Day Invasion. It went on to be used by various industries, including NASA. Even though it is a tool of the aerospace industry, it is not rocket science or difficult to develop a comprehensive and effective one. It simply requires focus and discipline.

To review the FMEA grasps the nature of $Y=f(x)$ and its impact on an output (Y) created by the variation of the process's inputs (Xs). By creating a risk assessment based on objectivity and a numeric assignment, it allows the list of possible failures to be prioritized.

Frequency, Severity, and Detectability

The core of the FMEA are the three factors that create risk. We define risk as the probability of an occurrence and its impact on that which is affected by the condition. Those three factors are:

- **Frequency—A rating based on the count of historical events occurring over a given period.**
- **Severity—A rating based on the impact to the organization and/or the customer.**
- **Detectability—A rating based upon the ability to identify the variation in the X before it impacts the output Y.**

The is not a standard set of assessment criteria. All three factors can vary according to the process. This is where the effort to obtain agreement begins. Many assume that what is being referred to is the ratings, but it is with the rating system itself. It is easier to edit than create. I would advise using the following factor criteria as the starting point. Developing the risk for any given input failure is the easy part! The second easiest effort is creating a list of all the inputs. The most difficult effort is identifying all the possible ways that an input can fail.

FREQUENCY			SEVERITY			DETECTABILITY		
Description	Numeric	Rating	Description	Numeric	Rating	Description	Numeric	Rating
Highest Probability	>41%	10	Extreme Impact		10	No Warning	0%	10
Very High Probability	36-40%	9	Very High Impact		9	Remote Chance	<5%	9
High Probability	31-35%	8	High Impact		8	Low Chance	6-10%	8
Moderate to High Probability	26-30%	7	Moderate Impact		7	Moderate Chance	11-15%	7
Moderate Probability	21-25%	6	Low Impact		6	Moderate Probability	16-20%	6
Low to Moderate Probability	16-20%	5	Very Low Impact		5	Chance	21-25%	5
Low Probability	11-15%	4	Minor Impact		4	Probability	26-30%	4
Very Low Probability	6-10%	3	Very Minor Impact		3	High Probability	31-50%	3
Rare Probability	2-5%	2	Some Impact		2	High Chance	51-99%	2
No Probability	<1%	1	No Impact		1	Certain	100	1

Starting with the categories, define each, then, if possible, support each level with data. A great example for Frequency could be the number of times that this occurs in a specific period. The important result of this activity is engagement and agreement on the ranking.

Once this is finalized, the inputs and their failure states are ranked, and the corresponding rating is loaded into the appropriate cells.

Process Step	Key Process Input	Potential Failure Mode	Potential Failure Effects	SEV	Potential Causes	FRE	Current Controls	DET	RPN
		Volume	Too little						0
		Volume	Too much						0
		Volume	Not at all						0
		Quality	Too little						0
		Quality	Too much						0
		Quality	Not at all						0
		Time	Too little						0
		Time	Too much						0
		Time	Not at all						0
		Cost	Too little						0
		Cost	Too much						0
		Cost	Not at all						0
									0

The focus at this point in the activity is to accurately complete the Severity, Frequency, and Detectability columns. You will note that there are two columns interlaced in this section of the analysis. Often during the development of the FMEA, individuals will suggest Causes and point out the current controls in place. These columns are there to capture them for later use.

This takes us to the RPN or Risk Priority Number. This is automatically calculated by the spreadsheet. After the Input assessment is completed, sort the entire spreadsheet, in descending order, based on this column. Doing so will place the highest risk errors on the top of the list. Once achieved, the FMEA now directly points to what process errors need to be addressed.

At this point the remaining areas on the FMEA focus on the changes made and the adjusted impact of the changes. This provides additional support to which errors to address in relation to the net change in risk. This can be calculated by subtracting the Adjusted Risk Priority Number from the initial Risk Priority Number. The equation for this is:

Net Risk Reduction Impact = ARPN—RPN

It is important to assess the project's focus based on a prioritized list (again in descending order).

This puts a close to our discussion on the FMEA. As with all of life's activities, you will receive value in direct relation to what you put into it. This single activity is often the most valuable effort, and based upon that fact alone, the FMEA should become a major activity.

5—IMPROVE

"Now that we know what is causing it, what are we going to do?" That is the purpose of the project phase, and it is appropriately named with the answer to that question, "Improve it!" The objective of this phase is to obtain agreement on the solution or solution set. There are numerous activities that can be aligned in it, but there are three major activities:

- Identify the solution or solution set
- Test and confirm the solution is effective with a pilot
- Develop and execute a change management plan

Once achieved, agreement will be easily obtained.

5A—ALTERNATE SOLUTIONS

Have you thought of everything? At the end of the I-phase, your project will be making a final recommendation. As it is with the previous phases, agreement is critical to project success. Knowing what to achieve agreement on is a great start. As you make a final recommendation, the response may be, "Have you considered . . .?" To contribute to our objective of agreement at every step in the DMAIC path, you need to be prepared, not only to make a case for your recommendation, but also explaining why the other solutions are not the best.

Alternate Solutions

Seldom is there a single solution to a problem. Given the many solutions available, selecting the best one is a matter of finding the greatest impact to reducing the frequency and severity of the occurrence at the lowest cost. Because Six Sigma is based on data-driven decision-making, knowing the specifics for each solution is critical so that the decision-makers can move to final implementation with the highest level of confidence.

Where can I find Alternative Solutions?

I learned a particularly important skill while working on my graduate degrees, that being the importance of literature searches. Back when I conducted literature searches, it was a manual process, using reference books, forms, printing, and the review of microfilm. Although it was difficult, I felt like I was an investigative reporter. The result of my work led to four filing cabinet drawers packed with material that I read and marked. I learned more about my topics because of this requirement. If I had the internet and the search engines that are now available, my work would have been significantly less labor-intensive and probably more thorough.

I learned something particularly important because of this work. Whatever the topic I researched, there was more information available than I had imagined. I understood with a profound depth the true meaning of the phrase, "There is nothing new under the sun."

The internet and search engines have made looking for answers significantly easier. There are numerous strategies that one can use to search for the answers. I suggest using multiple strategies and developing your own. Effective solutions are often found in the most obscure corners of the internet. Here are three of my most often used strategies that I use to search for alternative solutions:

- Copy and paste the problem statement in the search engine.
- Copy and paste the goal statement in the search engine.

Create a sentence that contains the words effective solution to removing (root cause).

Once Found, Then What?

Nothing is new under the sun. Someone has encountered the issue that your project is addressing in some form or another, and they have written about it. Dig into each solution with intensity and list them as alternatives within the I-phase of your project. Presenting a long list of alternatives within the project often addresses the "have you thought of or considered . . ." comment that is always waiting to make an appearance and rain on a great project parade. This is also where the recommendation can be justified. Remember to focus on the benefit and the cost. A third criteria to include whenever possible are the long-term consequences and impacts. In the end, your goal is to remove all options using data. Keep in mind this bit of advice, "If you find yourself in a position that you have to make a decision, you need more data." Having decided on the alternative, we are quickly moving toward testing for its true effectiveness.

5B—PREDICTED IMPACT

Having selected a recommendation from the options, the case needs to be made for your selection. This starts with a prediction of the impact that will result from the change. The costs and the benefits, both short-term and long-term. The goal is to show that what is recommended is a no-brainer and that the alternatives are not real options.

The underlying objective in every phase of a project is to obtain and maintain agreement. If agreement is questioned or lost, the project is on a path of failure. This requires a significant focus on the voice of the process owners or stakeholders. Let us recall our operational definition of a stakeholder; it is any individual affected by the change whose opposition can negatively impact the outcome of the change and not get fired.

The use of astute change management techniques become important at this juncture in a project. The successful change manager spends less time on promoting the benefits of the change and more time on addressing the concerns related to the change. Our assumption is that people do not resist change, they fear loss. Many projects fail because the fears related to the proposed change were not addressed. Often the fears are unwarranted, other times they are. Change management is always addressed with our Change Management Triad. The triad consists of the following:

- Stakeholder Analysis
- Influence Strategy
- Communication Plan

This effort will often lead to those characteristics of the project that need the highest level of emphasis, which addresses the concerns of the stakeholders. Project leaders often become myopic or tunnel-visioned because of their ownership of the results and their awareness of the vicious details related to the problem and the solution. They then assume that everyone knows and agrees. This is a bad assumption that can cause high levels of change resistance among the stakeholders.

The change management triad effort begins with a Stakeholder Analysis. It is a simple effort with the answer to three questions:

- Who are the project stakeholders?
- Where are they, related to the project?
- Where do they need to be to make this project successful?

Those three questions make more sense when you see the form that is used to document the analysis.

Stakeholder Analysis

Stakeholder Name & Title	Strongly Against	Moderately Against	Neutral	Moderately Supportive	Strongly Supportive
Tom (IT)	Present			Future	
Sam (IT)					Present
Ann (HR)				Present	Future
Sue (IT)					Present

Present = Where Stakeholder is now regarding the change

Future = Where Stakeholder needs to be for change to be a success

⎯⎯→ = Gap

- This tool ensures that you have considered the impact of the change on the people.
- This tool can be used at any stage of your project.

Once the stakeholders have been identified, the next step is to identify where they need to be, which ranges from Strongly Against to Strongly Support, to make the project a success. Considering Y=f(x), the level of support that each supply to the project is an input or X and critical to the success or Y of the project process. We often do not view our projects from the perspective of it being a process itself. Project success from this perspective reminds us that to achieve the objectives requires all of the inputs aligned and in the appropriate levels.

This takes us to the next activity important to Change Management, the Influence Strategy. This is an activity that is best accomplished by listening. It begins by briefly presenting the recommendation and focusing only on the change. Then asking, "What do you think of this proposal?" and listening to their feedback. This is powerful because you are asking for their insights. At the appropriate times during the conversation, the next question should be asked, "What would you do to address or fix this concern?" This information should be documented thoroughly because it feeds the next activity. The Influence Strategy is documented on a form that is like the following:

{PM: Insert image Influence Strategy-the partner}A separate form should be developed for each stakeholder to ensure that every concern is addressed. This leads to the last activity in the triad, the Communication Plan. Plans are great, but they are nothing until they become real! The first step in making them real is to put the plans on paper. I live by the axiom that says, "If it is not on paper, it's not real!" That may not be entirely true, but documentation is one step closer to reality. The communication plan captures the what? to who? where? And when? It is a project plan that helps ensure that all the X's related to project support and success are correct. Remember that every time an element is delivered there should follow a check to see if the stakeholder has changed their position related to the project support need. Messaging and communication should persist until the proper level of support is achieved. The communication plan should look like this:

Change Management Tool:
Communication Plan

This tool is optional in
Whitebelt.

Audience	Message	Media	Who Delivers Message	When	Where
Tom (IT)	Staffing has been increased	Verbal Documented	CFO	Quarterly Budget Review	Conference Room
Tom (IT)	Free Training for all Staff	Contract Review	Purchasing VP	10/27	War Room

Every potential concern needs to be tactically identified and addressed. This leads us to the topic at hand, which is predicting impact.

How do I Predict Impact?

Predicting impact is not a linear effort that follows the change management triad. It is integrated within it. Often the concerns that stakeholders raise are related to the true impact of the recommended change. It is all about risk. If you remember, risk is simply defined as the probability of it occurring as intended. If a stakeholder can be guaranteed that the change will have the intended impacts, there would be little to no resistance. Whenever resistance is encountered, it is indicative of a concern of risk. The job of a project leader is to identify and address those concerns. Often the project will be modified to address the insights provided by concerned and resistant stakeholders. That is a benefit related to project success. Do not be open to change. The goal of a project is to meet and exceed the expectations of the process owners and process customers while ensuring the change will continue as intended. To that end, knowing the Cause/Effect/Impact of the impact across all the process spectrum is important. It is not simply a cost/benefit analysis, but it can start there. To predict impact, the following elements need to be considered. The following is a partial list of categories to consider:

- Actual cost of change
  - Direct project cost
    - People
    - Process
    - Machinery
    - Management
    - Methods
    - Materials
  - Indirect costs to associated processes affected by the change
    - People
    - Process
    - Machinery
    - Management
    - Methods
    - Materials
    - Benefits of change
  - Product or service volume increase
  - Lost revenue
  - Increased revenue
  - Waste elimination costs

- In process rework cost elimination
  - Decreased Error Frequency
  - Decreased Error Severity/Impact
- Warranty cost elimination

Once Found, Then What?

I have found that most of the concerns expressed by the stakeholders will fall into the prior categories. This is not a complete list but acts as a starting point from which questions and discussions can be generated. If you have not noticed, this list of cost and benefit categories can be used to elicit concerns of stakeholders during the investigative stage of the change management triad.

When possible, the impacts predicted should be converted to their value in terms of dollar impact, both negative and positive. Those areas that have no monetary value should still be addressed as benefits or liabilities. All the items, monetary or nonmonetary, should be risk adjusted based on the frequency of their appearance in the successful process stream. What this means is that if half the time that the product is successful there are no returns from the customers, the total value of warranty returns is only half of its projected savings potential as compared to its full value, because half of the returns are not related to the error being addressed by the project.

Predicting the impact of the change accomplishes more than simply convincing the stakeholders that the project recommendation is viable. It also allows for a comparison of the predicted impact versus the goal or objective established in the Define phase, and it sets the bar for project closure at the end of the C-Phase. We can use the specific categories that are of major concern, including the original objects to create measures to validate project effectiveness and continuity.

If this is done correctly, I predict that the project is well on its way to success.

5C—TESTING AND PILOTING

Prove to me that it really works! This is often the only way that total agreement with the project's recommendation can be obtained. The short answer to this challenge is to run a pilot within the process and show how it performs. In many circumstances, this is not an option and the reason that many projects fail. Creative project leaders have another option to prove it works.

Pilot

The underlying objective in every phase of a project is to obtain and maintain agreement. If agreement is questioned or lost, the project is on a path of failure. This requires a significant focus on the voice of the process owners or stakeholders and addressing their concerns to their satisfaction. From the last discussion, we can recall our operational definition of a stakeholder as any individual affected by the change whose opposition can negatively impact the outcome of the change and not get fired. If a stakeholder is concerned the change in the process will not work, they will not agree with the recommendation. It is as simple as that.

Change management at this juncture is a matter of substantive proof, most often created through a pilot. When this option is available, it is recommended that it be conducted. Replicating the changes and measuring the performance in the process environment goes a long way to engaging the stakeholders in the change and quelling the concerns of the resistors.

It is often said that one should never burn bridges, leaving a way to return, if the return was needed. The pilot of the recommended change should be the last time that bridge or return to the original process is available. After the change is proven, the old way of doing things should be eliminated. Effective change management includes ensuring that once the changes are in place, the return to the original process generating the issues is impossible. We will address burning bridges in a future session. This will focus on the essential elements of an effective pilot. Adhering to the precepts of the scientific method, a successful pilot should follow as much of a controlled

The Elements of an Effective Pilot

- The pilot process should be as controlled as possible.
- If possible, the original process should be run in parallel to provide a comparative dataset.
- The Y output should be monitored for performance.
- All required X measures should be captured.
- A final report should be generated that provides a comparison of the pilot performance to the project objective.

The goal of a pilot is to provide information that confirms that the performance of the recommendations meets the objectives of the project or at minimum those that the change is projected to make. A successful pilot addresses the concerns of all the stakeholders. It is recommended that the concern and reasons for nonagreement be captured and they are addressed, either prior to the pilot start (when possible) or with information gathered during the pilot itself.

It is recommended that one uses the influence strategy form to compile the concerns and needs related to the pilot. This should be the foundation for the measurement system and the data provided by the pilot. There is one objective of the influence strategy at this juncture, that is to dispel the concerns or confirm them and adjust the recommendation to then address the change to the satisfaction of the stakeholders. The unspoken objective is to gain total support of the recommended change.

The Pilot and Influence Strategy

Keep in mind that every process improvement project is about change. Managing change is an important role of the project leader. If it is assumed that acceptance of the recommended change is a given, important aspects of the changes required may be missed. Hidden within the use of the Influence Strategy is the ability to find aspects that may have been overlooked.

Influence Strategy- the partner
tool of the Stakeholder Analysis

Stakeholder Name & Title	Issues/Concerns	Identify "Wins"	Influence Strategy
Tom (IT)	Additional Staffing	HR Support	Additional Staffing Approved
	Budget Increases	More Money to Support	CFO Approval
	Technology advancement	Free Staff Training	Contract by Provider

This tool helps you develop a strategy to influence
people to accept and support the change.

Tool is usually used when resistance is identified.
It can be used to enhance support when there is no resistance.

The Desktop Pilot

Piloting is critical to the unequivocal success of a project. So much so in fact that I could say that a project should not move forward without one. Realizing that I cannot make a statement like that without providing an alternative. The desktop pilot is an alternative when the data can support its use. What is a desktop pilot? Let us take a deep dive into the concept and make it a viable option.

- Original Process—$Y = f(X1, X2, X3, X4)$
  - The overall defect rate of this process = 26 percent
- Recommended Process—$Y = f(X1, \mathbf{X2}, X3, X4)$
  - The recommended change is a change in the X2 input.
  - Analysis during the A-phase points to process failures whenever the X2 component did not meet input requirements.
  - Additional analysis indicated a 1:1 correlation between X2 failures and a defect.
  - 74 percent of the time, when X2 met input requirements, the process provided an output that met customer requirements.

71

The logic used in this bullet point description is a simple way of laying out how a desktop pilot is conducted. It begins with a sizable data set, hopefully it is the same data set used in the analysis phase of the project. This data set contains data of process success and failures. The first analysis, which was already completed in the A-phase, was the overall defect rate. This was what was used to calculate the process sigma.

The next step is to sort out the entirety defects from the overall data set and ascertain the percent of the defects that contain the X2 failure. The closer to 100 percent for this number, the better. With the data set that contains only successes, the percentage of successes that exist that also contain an X2 failure is calculated. The closer to zero (0) the better.

Comparing the percentage of X2 failure correlations to the overall goal will guide the agreement of change as either the fulfillment of the objective or a partial fulfillment of it with a commitment to find and change the rest. As with an actual pilot, it is important to capture and present the data as support while entertaining the observations and concerns of the stakeholders.

Pilot Complete, Now What?

If a pilot is properly conducted, one has taken the observation of correlation to the next step, causation. Causation cannot be assumed but proven. If one finds a 100 percent relationship between an X and a Y, causation is then proven. Until this is done, only correlation can be assumed. Correlation is nice to know and can play in the predictive realm of process improvement, but when causation is found, real process improvement occurs. Therefore, I say that pilots are critically important to success. It is the icing on the cake of the scientific method and it completes the process itself with proof. There is not a stakeholder alive who would resist the change if it is proven, and that is what a pilot does.

6—CONTROL

This may be the final phase of the DMAIC project journey, but it is not the least important. The future effectiveness of the change and its continuation rests on how well the important steps within this phase are accomplished. The objective of this phase is to return full control and ownership of the new process to the stakeholders. To do so they need to agree to the change in its final form. Real change takes time. As we previously noted, we must ensure that they cannot and have not returned to the old ways. To do so, different measurement systems need to be put into place. Another important aspect is that everyone involved has received the necessary training to accomplish their assignments and tasks without fail.

If this is the first time that a DMAIC project has addressed an issue in this project, then there will be many new documents created. If this is a second-plus time, then the documentation will be edited and updated. Keep in mind that your project is focused on making changes for the better that last. This is your mission. In an interesting sense, this should be everyone's life mission.

This is the control phase in a nutshell, and it begins with a review of the exit strategy that was created and agreed upon at the beginning of the project. The C in DMAIC represents Control. I, however, prefer that it stands for Continuation. If the stakeholders agree to continue processing following the recommended and implemented changes, the project can be handed off and considered a success.

The final phase of a DMAIC project is not an afterthought. In some ways, it is as demanding as any other phase, and by design, it is the process seed that is planted that will grow into a weed or a plant that provides the intended harvest.

6A—EXIT STRATEGY REVIEW

Whenever I see a movie title that has the word "Reloaded" in its title, I know that it is going to be worse on the characters than the original. That is not the case with the reload of the Exit Strategy, in fact, it is a happily-ever-after, from the very beginning, if the previous phases of the project were properly conducted. As much fun as the project was, it is time to give it all back to the stakeholders and process owners. The C-phase begins with the review of the exit strategy and what was committed to in the very beginning.

Exit Strategy Reloaded

There is nothing better than hearing your project champion and process owner say, "WOW!" in reference to your work, or "I am glad you worked on this project!" The probability of hearing those words or some that carry a similar message are high if you accomplished the goals and objectives of each phase.

The exit strategy has clearly defined what completed and delivered looks and feels like. Staying consistent with the fact-based nature of the DMAIC problem-solving process, the exit strategy is supported with confirmed data. The goal and objective of the reload of the exit strategy is to confirm that all the requirements have been met. I know that it has been a while since we discussed Exit Strategy, so let us quickly review it.

The Exit Strategy

The project will be considered completed when the following elements have been addressed:

- TIME—A decrease in time or an established timeframe.
- QUALITY—A decrease in defects or a SIGMA increase in process performance.
- VOLUME—A volume increase.
- COST—A reduction in some process cost.

In preparation for the meeting, it important to review the original agreed-upon Exit Strategy document and ensure that all the goals and objectives documented have supporting data. More important is that the data show that each objective has been met or exceeded.

Only after the first step is satisfactorily completed and confirmed is the actual review meeting conducted. This is where the "happily" is given up front and the rest of this phase is focused on ensuring that the current performance will stay "ever after." Once you have reviewed the performance and have obtained agreement on the fact that the project has technically ended, the real value of the C-phase occurs.

6B—MEASUREMENTS AND MONITORING SYSTEMS

66 "That which cannot be measured cannot be managed" and "If it is not on paper, it is not real" are among the two gems of wisdom that can morph into a threat of failure if not properly completed during this final phase. Let us look at what we can do to avert that threat.

Measurements and Monitoring Systems

Often, one of the reasons causing the process problems that necessitated many of the projects that I have worked on has been a lack of a measurement system. At this point in the project, active and aligned measurement systems fulfill numerous requirements for closure and play an important role in the continuity of change. Let us review each:

C-Phase Measurement and Monitoring Requirements

- In an ongoing fashion, captures and displays the change in process improvement or waste reduction.
  - **Ensures the bridge has been burnt**
- In an ongoing fashion, captures and displays the control of the process inputs to reduce or eliminate substandard input into the process.
  - **Controls . . . Garbage in . . . Garbage out**
- In an ongoing fashion, captures and displays the relevant process performance metrics, allowing for process management of and reaction to errors before they become customer-impacting defects.
  - **Controls . . . "Errors cause defects"**
- Provides the unit impact that has occurred for the financial analysis.
  - **"It is not real until it is on paper!" . . . The "So What" of a project**

I know that you see that creating process and performance measures is not a checkbox item in the effort to finalize and hand off the project. It is the tool provided to the process owner that, if constructed properly, will make their job easier. Moreover, the measurement and monitoring system should perfectly align with and feed the Management, Reaction, and Disaster Recover plans. It should also have a detailed and descriptive data collection plan that itself is measured and monitored for compliance.

Creativity is the Key

I while back, we discussed the concept that a data collection plan is nothing more than the blueprint for a trap. The plan, in this instance, will be designed to control the recurrence of the root cause of the issues addressed in the project and control the other critical aspects that could affect sustainability. Creativity is critical during the development of this pan and the subsequent rollout of the measurement and monitoring system. As much as possible, it needs to run independently and not drain on process resources. It also needs to be in place prior to the project close. Nothing can kill the process changes quicker than a cumbersome measurement and monitoring system. This is when reverse engineering and creative development are put to the test.

Creating an Effective Measurement and Monitoring System

I mentioned that this measurement and monitoring system is reverse engineered. Let us look at the steps that will explain what I meant and the rationale behind it.

The Development and Implementation Path
- Measure Identification
  - The important output measures and their sources of data
  - The critical inputs and their sources of data
  - The critical process measures and their sources of data
- Develop and validate data collection plans related to each data source

- Develop and test collection and documentation procedures
- Train and pilot data capture and display
- Review effectiveness and costs
  - Time
  - Labor
- Adjust from Pilot Discoveries
- Repeat Pilot

This concept maintains consistency with our process equation, $Y=f(x)$. Remember that a defect is a condition of the process output that does not meet the recipient's requirements. An error in the development of the measurement system is twofold. First and foremost, the users need to see the value of the measurement system and know how to use it. Second, the users need to agree that the measuring effort is worth it. Because a process is a series of tasks or activities that changes in how they accomplish their objectives, the addition of a measurement system can be perceived as a hindrance. Being aware of this tendency, obtaining the agreement of the users is critical. Listening and responding to each concern and objection is important to achieving closure and success.

Once agreement on the measurement system and its integration to the process is obtained, it is time to move to final closure. This is not only an important part of making change real, but also important to the real handoff of the process to the owners. Process measurements and monitoring systems are not an afterthought. They are a critical part of processing and continuous improvement.

We have covered the most critical characteristics of creating a successful measurement and monitoring system. Many practitioners do not need measurement and monitoring systems as a part of the process. Carrying the message that these are the control part and will ensure consistency of delivery is an important role of the project leader. As it always seems to be the case, there is always more that could be addressed, but please allow me to remind you that if you need guidance and assistance, the Cii team of experts can help. You can get more information at www.thecii.com

6C—BPM PROCESS CONTROL PLANS

"It is a plan!" You have probably heard that said and thought in response, "That is just another baseless statement!" Sadly, you were probably correct! If it is not on paper, it is not real. Control plans are a critical deliverable that drives agreement in the final phase of a Six Sigma project. Traditional training falls short of the complete documentation required to obtain agreement and ensure that the change will last.

Control Plans

It is said that great things come in threes. This could not be truer when it comes to the Control phase of a Six Sigma project. From my perspective, control is somewhat a misleading term to describe this phase. I prefer continuation because that is what we are seeking in terms of the agreement that we seek from the stakeholders and process owners.

To achieve that we must do our homework and borrow some activities from Business Process Management, which is often referred to as BPM. I would prefer that an entire Business Process Management be developed for every process; I also must be realistic! At this point I suggest that the process control planning and response system be developed and implemented. It consists of the following three plans:

The Process Control Plans

- Management Plan
- Reaction Plan
- Disaster Recovery Plan

Many ask, "Isn't one plan enough?" My response is that there are three conditions of a process at any given time. For each of the conditions, we have a plan guiding the appropriate response. Let us go a bit deeper and get a thorough understanding of each and why they are separate and needed to ensure continuity of the project change. Let us begin with data and a significant control chart related to the process.

The question that should be asked of the most current data point is, "How is the process doing?"

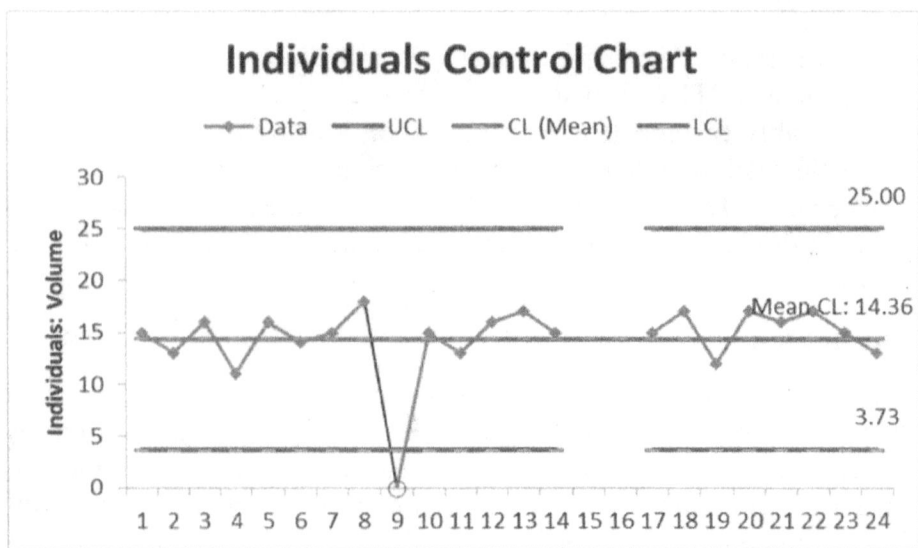

This chart has all three process states represented on it. Let us look at each.

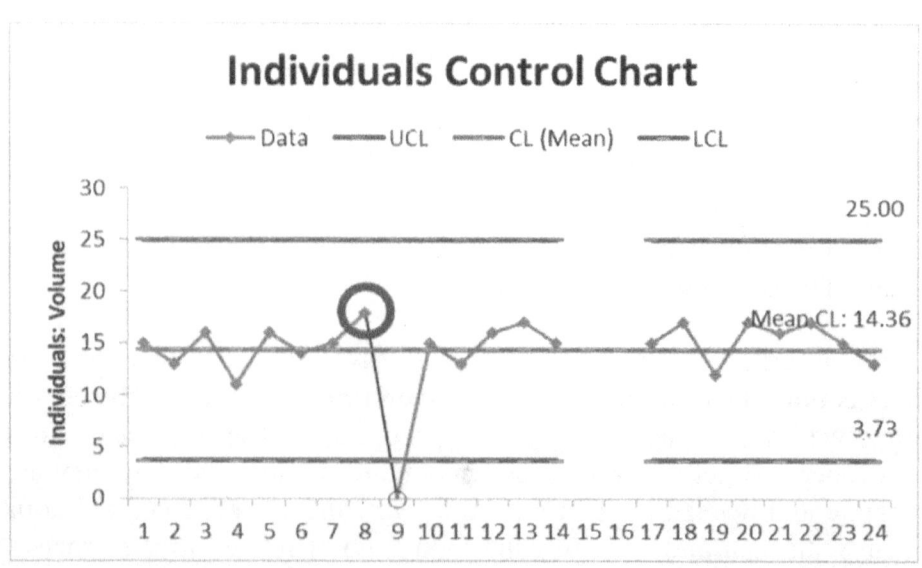

This data point is within the control limits and the appropriate answer is, "The process is in control and we are managing." The appropriate activity is to keep doing what the management plan has spelled out. This is the Management Plan.

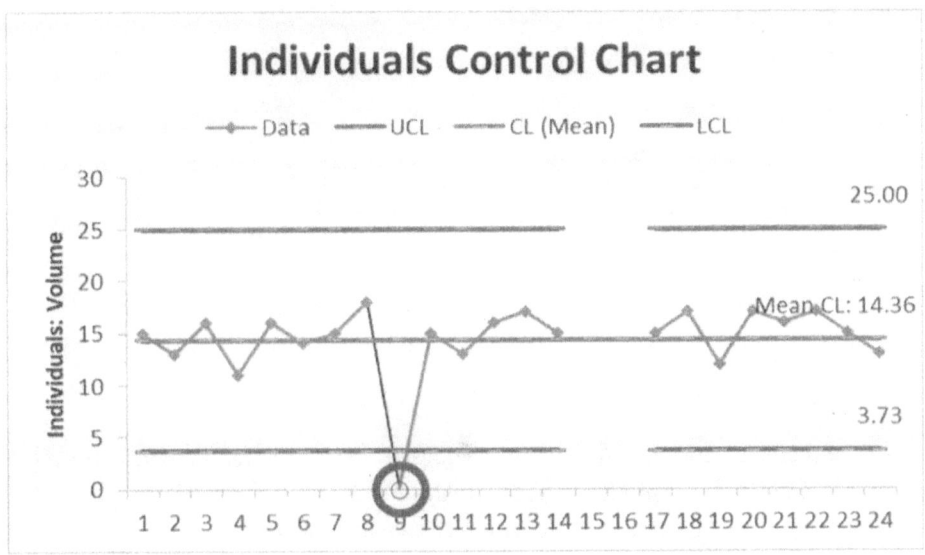

In this situation the data indicates a performance that is outside of the control limits. The answer to the question should be, "We are reacting to bring the process back into control." In some situations, the data may indicate a situation exceeding the upper control limit. If this situation is favorable, as it is in this case, the response is, "We are performing way above expectations. We are looking into the reasons why and will see if this can become the performance in the future." The plan related to what to do when the process is out of control is the Reaction Plan. It directs the operational people on how to react in these situations.

The data in this next chart . . . Wait, there is no data point! This is correct! When a process is generating no data, it is a disaster! What to do in this situation is spelled out in a disaster recovery plan. In most instances, the lack of data is a result of the process not performing. The disaster recovery plan usually directs the relevant personnel on how to recover or restart a process.

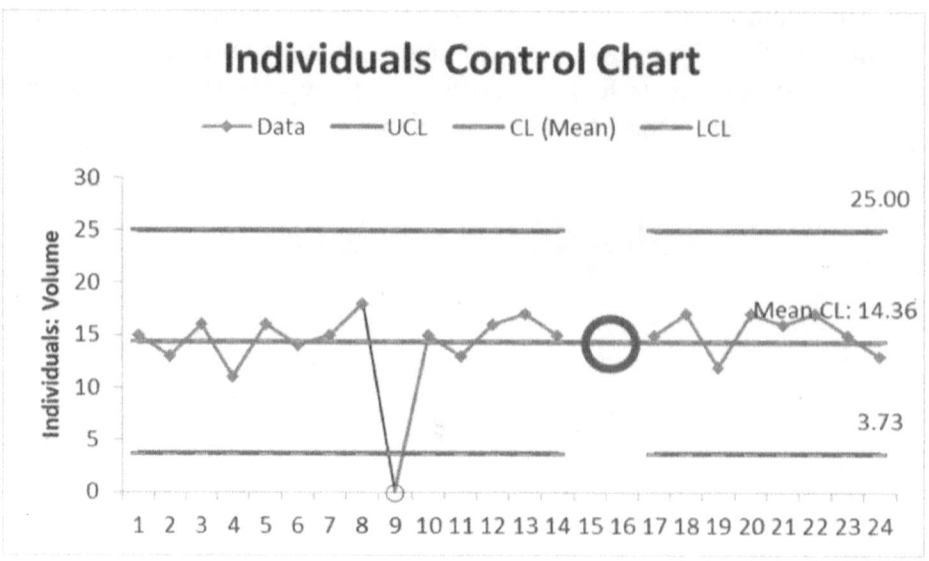

When asked during this phase in the process whether a comprehensive Process Control Plan has been created? The affirmative response requires all three of these plans and the rationale behind them.

The Plans

- Management Plan—Which guides and directs how to keep the process performing within control.
- Reaction Plan—How to respond when the process goes out of control, bring performance back into expectations, or maintain the improved performance when it exceeds performance expectations.
- Disaster Recovery Plan—What to do when the process totally fails.

Finishing a project is more than breathing a sigh of relief. There are many Ts to cross and Is to dot. What makes or breaks a project at this point is inattention to details. The starting point is a Process Control Plan that works. If the three are done correctly, they become a good thing!

6D—UPDATED PROCESS DOCUMENTATION

In the beginning of the project, I have made it a habit to ask if there is existing process documentation. When the answer is yes, I ask to see it. Often, they reach into a drawer or take a binder off a shelf and figuratively blow the dust off of it! If you have not figured out where I am going with this, it is an indicator of one of the sources of the problem! At the end of a project, I ask if the process documentation has been updated.

Control Plans

You have heard me say it before, I will say it again, "If it is not on paper, it is not real!" With process change continuity being the objective of this phase of the DMAIC project, providing a proverbial first step ensured that what has been changed will remain that way. If left to itself, a process will return to the old ways of doing things, that is, if the bridges are not burned, and the participants are not enmeshed in the new ways supported by the owners and stakeholders.

Process documentation is crucial to continuity. It is the rule book, even many will call it a playbook to euphemize its importance. Documentation is not a standard template. Depending on the process and the audience, it can contain a plethora of documents. Adaptation to the audience is at the core of effectiveness. It is the thing to remember and should act as guidance in the development of effective documentation. Also, keep in mind a concept that we discussed earlier, which is that individuals communicate in one of three ways, verbally, numerically, or visually. To that end, important documentation should and will meet the understanding needs of one or more of the audiences. Ultimate effectiveness is achieved when nearly anyone can pick up the documentation and perform the task assigned at the prescribed error rate.

What is inside Effective Process Documentation?

Developing or revising process documentation begins with this question to the users: "What do you need to do your job flawlessly?"

This question should be asked of everyone involved with the process, remembering that not everyone has the same communication needs. Using their answers, a table of contents can be developed, and from this, the documentation can be created.

Although this is not a comprehensive list of contents, the following are what is regularly found in a complete process documentation set:

- Process Introduction—Reviews the purpose of the process from beginning to end, with a focus on the specific customer requirements (CTQs). Other measurable performance characteristics can include:
  - Time
  - Volume
  - Quality
  - Cost
- A list of the process measures
  - Input measures and related specification limits
  - In-process measurements and tolerances
  - Output measures and goals/objectives
- A current SIPOC that details the process inputs
- Process Flow maps (Task level preferred over functional)
- Standard Operating Procedures for each task
- A current FMEA
- Data collection plans to support the previously noted measures
- Process plans
  - Management
  - Reaction
  - Disaster Recovery

It is straightforward and easily accomplished if the phase documentation was properly assembled during the previous phases. I have watched many brilliant and effective changes revert to the former defective process because there was no documentation of the new process, and the excuse used was, "They didn't know!" I noted earlier that this is the first step. We will discuss its use in closing the final phase of your project later. Our goal is to remove every and any excuse for not conforming to the new process, giving them no alternative but to do it the new way.

6E– NEW PROCESS TRAINING

Amazing documentation is totally worthless if no one uses it. It is impossible to ensure the ongoing use of it, but you can ensure the process owners and stakeholders that everyone has seen every word, diagram, and number on every page. How? First, by identifying every reason or excuse that could be used to not know the process documentation. Then, by including training as part of your C-phase project closure. After effective training and messaging, noncompliance can be likened to insubordination, which adds to the motivation to do it the new way!

The Important Pieces in the Process Training Puzzle

Effective training involves creating a perfect storm with three major components:

- **Students**—Individuals who have a compelling reason for being in attendance and are motivated to learn.
- **Teachers**—Individuals who can effectively communicate the material to each student and are able to answer every question to the satisfaction of the student or get the answers for them.
- **Material**—Information that is understood by each student and supports the objective of the class.

When they intersect, it looks like this:

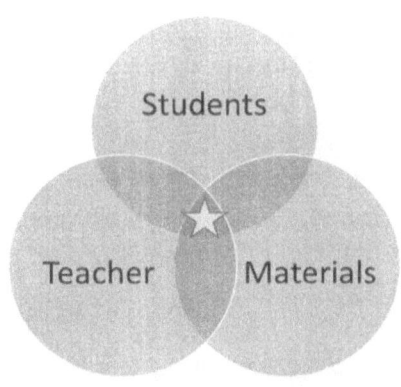

Ensuring that the importance and value of the change is conveyed and emphasized along with adhering to the process documentation, the priority is the selection and preparation of the teachers or facilitators. You will notice that I pluralized the training leaders. Process owners should, when possible, lead the training. They should give their endorsement of the change and emphasize the value to everyone. Most process owners are not good teachers, so their involvement should be limited to the introduction and overview of the change and emphasis.

The instructor or facilitator that follows the introduction needs to be well versed in the change. A great instructor also recognizes the need to communicate to three different audiences. Diving a little deeper into the prior statement, effective communication occurs across an audience comprised of three different styles. They are:

Communication Styles

- **Verbal Communicators**—These individuals gain understanding through words, verbal images, and stories.
- **Numeric Communicators**—These individuals gain knowledge through numeric relationships. They are concerned with cost/benefits.
- **Visual Communicators**—These individuals need to see pictures and drawings. They live in a world where a picture is worth a thousand words!

Content should be developed with all three styles taken into consideration. If a presentation is only graphs and charts, communication and understanding will only occur with numeric communicators. If the training session is just lecture, only the verbal communication style will be placated, and so on. The materials created in the prior phases of DMAIC should support this with little or no alteration.

The final piece of the puzzle is the selection of students. There are three mistakes often made in this situation. Too few people in attendance, too many people in attendance, and the wrong people in attendance. Care should be taken to identify everyone that needs to be trained has received that training. Often, this requires multiple classes to address the excuse that the session is inconveniently scheduled.

If process change is not thoroughly communicated, it will fail, and the excuse of, "I didn't know" is valid. Training is a powerful and essential part of change management. When the process owner asks, "Have all the people involved been properly trained?" the answer needs to be an enthusiastic, "Yes!" Our goal is to remove every and any excuse for not conforming to the new process, giving them no alternative but to do it the new way. Training is one way to take the excuses away.

6F—FINANCIAL REVIEW

"So What?" The first words out of the mouth of the CFO at a project review. Knowing that question was coming at every review brought high levels of anxiety to me until I engaged him as the owner of the review, and then the tables were turned!

Financial Review

The question "So what?" is a valid one! It requires justification for everything that has been put into the effort. It is a final assessment of the value related to process improvement and its impact across the entire organizational spectrum and assesses the intended consequences and the unintended consequences. The bottom line of value is truly the bottom line or net impact. The net impact should align with the goals and objectives that were established in the very beginning of the project when agreement was obtained with the exit strategy. In the C phase, the purpose of the official financial review is an independent certification of the required impact of the project. Without this certification, gaining agreement that the project met requirements and objectives is nearly impossible.

Revisiting the Exit Strategy

Although I have not emphasized this aspect of project management prior to this, as much as possible, a great project leader remains unbiased. I used to say that a great project leader acts like Sweden! Stay neutral and depend on data to guide your decisions. The financial review should assess all the costs (-) and tangible benefits (+) in terms of dollars and only dollars (repeated for emphasis). Intangible costs and benefits are for another meeting and have no place in this review. Keep it focused on the financial value to the company or organization. This is where the Exit Strategy comes into play. If you recall, the Exit Strategy focuses on the deliverables of the project in terms of four possible characteristics:

- Time—The net change needed in some characteristic of time. An example is a reduction of processing time of fifteen minutes per unit.
- Volume—The net change needed in some characteristic of volume. An example is an increase in products of 25 percent.
- Quality—The net change needed in some product or service quality characteristic. An example is a reduction in the identified defects of one sigma or 50 percent improvement within a product or service.
- Cost—The net change needed in some cost characteristic. An example is a reduction in waste that improves the overall cost of production.

If you have not noticed, each of these general categories has a word in common, "net." Remember that every change in a process has a cost associated with it. The purpose of the financial review is to add up the costs incurred related to the change, subtract them from the benefits derived, and present the "net" impact for each. A successful Financial Review presents numbers that meet or exceed the initial or adjusted expectations. If the project was run properly, any anticipated change was adjusted, presented, and agreed upon immediately after discovery. This makes a Financial Review simply a matter of formal closure because all those involved with the project already are aware of the results.

What does the Financial Review look like?

The Cost of Poor Quality Template (see next page)

Remembering that the Financial Review is a cost/benefit analysis, the starting point begins with an assessment of the costs associated with the defective state and a comparison of the performance of the changed state. I have found it most effective to use this spreadsheet twice; once for current or defective state and once for new state. The difference in the two sheets is the net impact. A cost per unit or activity can be applied, and the project value is generated.

It is important to note that this sheet is a template and should be modified to meet the exact needs of the project. Lines should be deleted

Process Name:
Process #:

Cost Of Poor Quality (COPQ)

Cost of Poor Quality (COPQ). Quantification of the revenue loss or additional cost associated with a defect. COPQ will align the defect volume to the profit impact to the business.

Defect Type

Define Defect Scope
- 'SIPOC' Input
- 'SIPOC' Output

Internal / External process Impacted from defects

Failure Cost

Appraisal cost: The cost to appraise or evaluate work other than the person performing the work.

Appraisal Cost	Dept	Dept Mgr	Defect Definition	Description of Cost	Cost / Defect	Assumptions
Product / Service / Process						
Product / Service / Process Audit						
Product / Service / Process Testing						
<Input Other>						

Internal failure cost: Costs associated with defects found internally before the customer identifies defect.

Internal Failure Cost	Dept	Dept Mgr	Defect Definition	Description of Cost	Cost / Defect	Assumptions
Redesign						
Rework						
Penalties						
Delays						
Downtime (Idle time)						
Loan write-off						
Customer compliant contact - phone						
<Input Other>						

External failure cost: Costs associated with defects found by the customer

External Failure Cost	Dept	Dept Mgr	Defect Definition	Description of Cost	Cost / Defect	Assumptions
Redesign						
Rework service / product						
Penalties						
Delays						
Downtime (Idle time)						
Loan write-off						
Customer compliant contact - phone						
<Input Other>						

Loss of Revenue: Defect triggers the loss of revenue

Loss of Revenue	Dept	Dept Mgr	Defect Definition	Description of Loss of Revenue	Cost / Defect	Assumptions
Student doesn't start						
Student drops						
Student doesn't attend future courses						
Money cost (Bank Interest or cost to						
Reduction of student referrals						
<Input Other>						
Total Failure Cost / Loss of Revenue per Defect					$	

Prevention costs: Prevention costs are costs of all activities that are designed to prevent poor quality from arising in products or services.

Prevention Cost	Dept	Dept Mgr	Defect Definition	Description of Cost	Annual Cost	Assumptions
Training						
Quality planning						
Quality improvement team meetings						
Quality improvement projects						
Dashboard creation						
New product / service review						
Vendor / System evaluation						
<Input Other>						
Annual Total Prevention Cost					$	

and added in each category as needed. At this point the Financial Review is half over! The last part is related to the actual project costs related to the change. Remember that changes do not occur without a cost. Software upgrades, the addition of personnel, change in machinery tooling, the cost of project leadership, etc., are all factors necessary for change and were a result of the project. The question to be answered with this part is, "If the project did not occur, would the cost have been incurred?"

When these parts are completed, a final document can be created. Subtracting the new state from the defective state should result in positive values. Multiplying this number by the cost per unit and the annualized volume will provide a dollar benefit provided by the project. Then subtracting the costs of change from the dollar benefits provides the net benefit. If these numbers meet or exceed the expectations of the exit strategy, the project is golden and another step toward closure and continuity has been achieved.

Financial Reviews are an important part of closing a single project. They are also an important part in ensuring the process improvement efforts continue to be supported within an organization. If every process improvement project meets and exceeds the expectations of the Exit Strategy and had a net positive financial impact, more projects can be anticipated, and that is the unspoken objective of any and every process improvement professional.

6G—THE FORMAL HANDOFF

The last word is seldom the last word when it comes to a project. In our case, we seek four words: "I agree" and "thank you."

The Formal Handoff

This is the moment that all project leaders look forward to with anticipation and, without fail, many project leaders close projects with a sense of sadness and loss. Feelings aside, every project has a life, a beginning and an end. Project closure opens doors to new opportunities. Great projects need to be closed properly. Many project leaders focus during the first four stages of DMAIC and conduct the C-phase as an afterthought. This is a big mistake. The C-phase is critical to continuity. It needs to be accomplished with the same level of attention to detail as the previous phases. This is what a great project leader does.

C-Phase Handoff

The objective of the C in C-phase has been called control. I prefer to call it continuity. The reason for calling it control is that in the past, most projects focused on controlling variation. I agree with that, but I also believe that control is inherent in the change, and the focus needs to be on the continuity of the change that has been implemented.

The handoff meeting is a formal exercise that ensures and validates agreement of the value of the efforts and agreement that the change is the way the process will be handled. To get that, the following project walk across should be followed:

Handoff Meeting Content
- Review Straight Talk
- Review Exit Strategy
- Review Recommendation and its implementation
- Review Measures and process control plans

- Review unit and financial impact
- Answer questions and complete signoff on charter

The actual content from a handoff meeting may vary from the list. Remember that the meeting is to get the users to agree that the project is complete. It may be appropriate to ask the attendees what they need to close the project. Use the list as a starting point and adjust as is appropriate.

Conducting the Meeting

If you have kept your project deck up to date during your project, the rest of the project should go easily. Schedule the meeting, welcome the participants, and begin with, "This is most likely the last meeting that we will have related to this project. The goal of the get-together is to return the control of the change and better performing process to you and answer any questions or concerns that anyone may have."

C is also for Celebrate!

After the formality, there is one more meaning to C-phase that I include and hopefully before anyone has left the meeting. It is "Let's Celebrate"! Organizations seldom take time to sufficiently celebrate success. Sadly, the celebrations that do happen sound like a sigh of relief, and then whoever is present runs off and fights another battle. I live with the saying "Never be the reason for someone's thankless day" in mind when I am involved in project closure. People tend to repeat engagements with efforts where they are recognized and appreciated. This sets the stage for future success. Other celebration discussions can include the war stories and how individuals overcame the challenges that stood between them and success. Whatever way you celebrate, the important thing is to celebrate. Do not miss an opportunity to do so, because in the project world it is a rare event.

Let us move on to the Next Challenge

Formally closing the project has occurred, and it is time to move to the next challenge. If you accomplished everything that your champion and owners needed you to do, you will have numerous highly complementary references. Humbly accept them and use them as needed. You are building a network of support that will make your overall job easier and your future more secure.

We have covered the most critical characteristics in managing a project to completion, of creating a successful measurement and monitoring system. There is one more important exercise before a project can be closed in the mind of the project leader. It is called Lessons Learned. We will address that in the next discussion. Always keep in mind that you are carrying the message of continuous improvement and that the project that is closing still has room for improvement. As always seems to be the case, there is more that could be addressed, but please allow me to remind you that if you need expert guidance and assistance, the Cii team can help. You can get more information at www.thecii.com

6H—LESSONS LEARNED

My mentor routinely reminded me, "You win some, or you learn something. In either case, get a prize." The grand prize related to a completed project, whether it was entirely successful or an utter failure, is what we call the Lessons Learned. It is a formal review and documentation of everything important to the project. If you do not do Lessons Learned, the project did not deliver what it was meant to deliver for you!

Lessons Learned

The Lessons Learned document is simply a bullet point list of important observations noted during the project. It can be created alone or by the project team. Its content should be comprehensive and contain the proverbial good, the bad, and the ugly! It documents:

- What you will avoid doing in the future and how to avoid it
- What you will repeat in the future and how to repeat it
- Important information specific to the process
- Future opportunities for projects

It can contain other pieces of information, but the purpose is to put on paper the experience you obtained during DMAIC. Remember, "It is not real if it is not on paper." This does not mean that a paper copy is required. It means that it must be amassed on a slide or slides or within some data-retention program. I have a specific folder called Lessons Learned in the cloud, in which documents are kept, each named for the project. If I were to do it over, I would create a single document, not unlike a journal, in which all my Lessons Learned would be documented. The choice is yours, because this is not part of the project but part of your career experience that supports your efforts in continuous improvement. My advice is to focus on your own continual improvement so that you are always ready for the next challenge. This is not just for your career, but it also serves your life.

Phillip C. Reinke

POST-PROJECT FOLLOW-UP

M any practitioners breathe a heavy sigh of relief at the completion of a project and vow to never return. The fact of the matter is that project follow-up is an important responsibility of a project leader to establish and verify change continuation. The frequency of follow-up often is informally weekly for a month or two, then monthly and finally quarterly over the course of a year. For changes to be instilled they must become habits. If individuals believe that the new process is being watched, they will perform as they believe they should, acting as prescribed. This is called the Hawthorne Effect. Change is a difficult thing, yet there are open doors within the human psyche that allow for it to happen. A great project leader performs as if their project comes with a guarantee of performance. Follow-up monitoring of all the critical activities and measurements helps them build that reputation and make that appearance a reality.

Review Requested:
We'd like to know if you enjoyed the book. Please consider leaving a review on the platform from which you purchased the book.